THE MARSHALL CAVENDISH
☆ ☆ ☆ ILLUSTRATED ☆ ☆ ☆
ENCYCLOPEDIA OF
WORLD WAR II

VOLUME 22

THE MARSHALL CAVENDISH
☆ ☆ ☆ ILLUSTRATED ☆ ☆ ☆
ENCYCLOPEDIA OF
WORLD WAR II

Based on the original text by
Lieutenant Colonel Eddy Bauer

CONSULTANT EDITOR

Brigadier General James L. Collins, Jr., U.S.A.

CHIEF OF MILITARY HISTORY,
DEPARTMENT OF THE ARMY

MARSHALL CAVENDISH CORPORATION/NEW YORK

CONTENTS

Editorial Director: Brian Innes
Editor-in-chief; Brigadier Peter Young, D.S.O., M.C., M.A.
Managing Editor: Richard Humble
Editor: Christopher Chant
Art Editor: Jim Bridge

CHAPTER 175

Victory in Burma

by Brigadier Michael Calvert

Previous page: *Machine gunners on Pagoda Hill during the battle for Fort Dufferin, Mandalay. This immensely strong fortress, which was surrounded by a moat 40 feet wide, had walls measuring 23 feet high and 30 feet thick (each one was a mile in length). The 19th Indian Division began its assault on March 8, but the Japanese 60th Regiment held out under fierce and almost constant bombardment until the 20th.*
△ *Advancing slowly southward through the Kaladan valley, a supply column of the 81st West African Division winds its way along a jungle track.*

Subjective 14th Army historians often neglect the Allied fighting forces which operated on either side of their advance and give the impression that it was the 14th Army alone who confronted the Japanese armies when they advanced down from Imphal to Mandalay and Rangoon. This, of course, was not the case and it was the Northern Combat Area Command under Stilwell with his three and then five Chinese divisions, coupled with first the Chindit operations and then the operations of the British 36th Division which first penetrated the plains of north Burma and turned the flank of the Japanese 15th Army facing the 14th Army. The ill-equipped 12 Chinese divisions on the River Salween have been denigrated for their lack of initiative and attacking spirit. But it must be remembered that these particular Chinese divisions each amounted to only a weak British brigade in strength, and from their point of view they were hundreds of miles away in a remote corner of China, facing one of the swiftest and most incalculable rivers in the world, the Salween, while the best armies and technical weapons available were being used to combat the 25 Japanese divisions occupying eastern and

central China. Whilst the operations described here were going on, the Japanese, incensed by American air attacks from China on shipping in the South China Sea and as far north as Japan itself, attacked and overran the Chinese provinces of Kwangsi and Hunan, an area about the size of France. It must also be remembered that the objectives given to Mountbatten and Stillwell for 1944, to which Stilwell stuck, as he felt that they must govern all his actions, was the capture of Mogaung and Myitkyina and an area south sufficient to protect those two towns, so that a road and petrol pipeline could be opened to China and help keep her in the war. Stilwell had responsibilities to China as well as South-East Asia.

General Giffard had judged that the Arakan coastal terrain was an area in which it was uneconomic to operate and had, therefore, decided to stop any further attempt to advance there. But when Mountbatten, who was still without sufficient landing craft to capture Rangoon, was given permission to conquer Burma from the north, he found that he was faced with a big logistic problem. Once the 14th Army, with its 260,000 troops, crossed the Irrawaddy, their communications to a railhead and air bases in Assam lengthened to such an extent that they became uneconomic. It was, therefore, necessary to capture and develop airfields along the coast of Burma which could be supplied easily by sea, so that Slim's 14th Army could in turn be supplied from there by air. Thus plans were made to expand the port and airfields at Chittagong and to capture Akyab and Ramree Islands, where airfields could be developed.

The 14th Army had started to cross the Chindwin early in December 1944 and Major-General T. W. Rees's 19th Indian Division, which had never been in action before, quickly crossed the formidable Zibyu Taungdan Range and made contact at Wuntho on the railway with Festing's British 36th Division, which was on a two brigade animal transport/jeep basis.

Slim, who appeared not to have been following the wider picture of operations in Burma and did not seem to appreciate the effect of Stilwell's advance, at first imagined that the Japanese would hold a line from Kalewa along the Zibyu Taungdan Range, which was immediately in front of his 14th Army. But Rees's rapid advance and link-up with Festing gave him information that the Japanese were not going to hold any area in force east of

the Irrawaddy. Slim had made extensive plans for an operation which he had called "Capital", whose objective was to capture the area west of the Irrawaddy. As soon as he realised that the advance of Stilwell's forces had made the Japanese face two ways, Slim made a new plan.

This new plan was called "Extended Capital". It must be realised here that each successive plan had not only to be devised and approved by both the 11th Army Group and South-East Asia Command planners in Calcutta and Ceylon respectively, but also had to obtain the agreement of first the Chiefs-of-Staff in London and then the Combined Chiefs-of-Staff in Washington, with the hope that Chiang Kai-shek in Chungking would also agree. This complicated planning procedure, although it was necessary to ensure that men, stores, weapons, and equipment were made available and that there would be some co-ordination between the four Supreme Commanders, Mountbatten, Chiang Kai-shek, Mac-Arthur, and Nimitz, fighting the Japanese war, both tended to delay operations and often failed to catch up with events. So Slim carried on ahead of approval.

"Extended Capital", in brief, entailed a fairly direct advance by Lieutenant-General M. G. N. Stopford's XXXIII Corps from Kalewa via Yeu and Monywa onto Mandalay, but included a left-hook with Rees's 19th Division crossing the Irrawaddy and advancing down the left bank on to the town of Mandalay itself. In this way XXXIII Corps could keep in touch with Stilwell's N.C.A.C.

The second and most important part of "Extended Capital" was for IV Corps (Lieutenant-General F. W. Messervy) to move due south down the Gangaw valley towards Pauk and Pakokku below the confluence of the Chindwin and Irrawaddy, cross the Irrawaddy, and advance due east on to the rail, road, and air communications centre of Meiktila. This change of plan meant some swapping of divisions between XXXIII Corps and IV Corps, but this was quickly done on paper.

The 14th Army would now, during the fine weather, be debouching into the dry zone of Burma where the "going" was good for armour and the air forces had good visibility for ground attack on troops and their communications.

A 1,150-foot Bailey bridge was built over the Chindwin at Kalewa and XXXIII Corps, consisting of the British 2nd

△ Campaigning in the jungle meant using whatever means were available – or capable of coping with the conditions. Jeeps were a luxury, mules the more usual form of transport. When the mules gave out, troops resorted to manpower – as the Royal Welch Fusiliers do here, crossing the Nanyke Chaung.

Division, the 20th Indian Division, the 254th Indian Tank Brigade, and the 268th Indian Infantry Brigade, advanced with deliberation towards Yeu and Shwebo in the north and Monywa and Myinmu in the south, with the 19th Division, also under command, crossing the Irrawaddy and causing the initial threat to Mandalay.

IV Corps under Messervy decided to make the 28th East African Brigade and the locally recruited "Lushai" Brigade be the vanguard of his corps down the Gangaw valley, with a cover plan that they were another Chindit-type penetration force moving around the Japanese flanks. Behind them would move the hard-hitting 7th and 17th Indian Divisions and the 255th Indian Tank Brigade.

By February 1, 1944, XXXIII Corps was on the right bank of the Irrawaddy. By February 13, IV Corps was reaching its jumping-off positions along the Irrawaddy, south of Myinmu. Meanwhile it would be opportune to review how the Japanese saw the situation and how the operations taking place on both flanks of the 14th Army affected their advance.

After the failure of the "HA-GO" offensive, some changes were made in the Japanese command. Lieutenant-General

H. Kimura replaced M. Kawabe as commander of the Burma Area Army. Lieutenant-General S. Katamura took over command of the 15th Army from R. Mutaguchi, who was sent home in disgrace but, in spite of Sato's threat, he was never court-martialled.

Kimura's orders were to cover the strategic areas of Burma as his main job, but, without prejudice to this task, to try to interrupt if possible Allied communications with China. He still had three armies under command and, with the arrival of the 49th Division from Korea, these numbered a total of ten divisions and two independent mixed brigades. But these figures give no indication of the real strength of his force. For instance, the four divisions making up the 15th Army, which had been largely destroyed in north Burma and Imphal, now numbered only 21,400 men. This total was split up between the 53rd Division from Mogaung (4,500), 31st Division (7,000), 33rd Division (5,400), and 15th Division (4,500). These numbers included artillery regiments with less than half their complement of guns, and other ancillary units.

Against this 15th Army strength of 21,000 men, plus a few local reinforce-

△ A British Stuart light tank moves up for the final assault on Fort Dufferin in Mandalay.
▷△ Two members of the Burma police interrogate villagers during the hunt for Japanese stragglers near Mandalay.
▷▽ A Bailey bridge being assembled in sections, later to be floated to the crossing point for the 14th Army.
▷▽▽ 62nd Motorised Brigade advances along the Myingyan-Meiktila road.
▽ The advance to Mandalay.

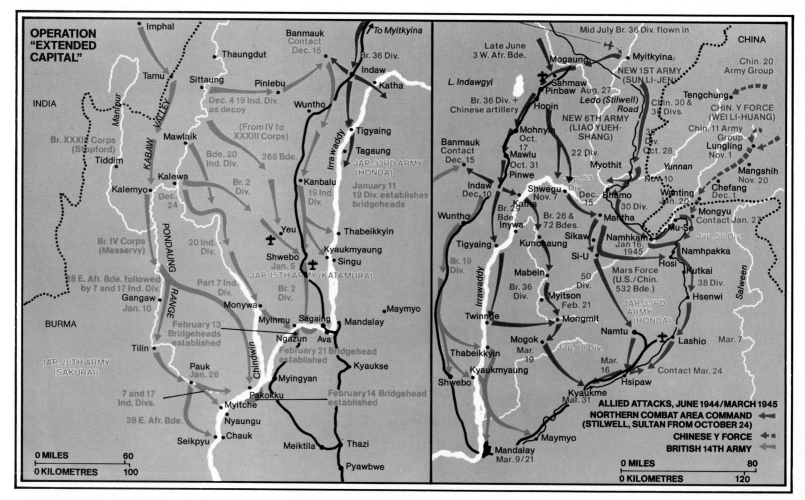

ments and corps and army troops, Slim's 14th Army of six divisions, two independent brigades, plus the lines of communication troops east of the Chindwin and two tank brigades, totalled a ration strength of 260,000 men. With this overwhelming superiority, tactics were not so important for victory as the logistics of manoeuvring such a force into position when so far away from reliable bases.

On the Northern and Salween fronts, Stilwell's five Chinese divisions (kept efficiently up to strength), the British 36th Division, "Mars" Force, (successors to Merrill's Marauders) and the 12 Chinese divisions in Yunnan, were faced by Lieutenant-General M. Honda's 33rd Army, consisting of the 18th, 56th, and 49th Divisions, and the 24th Independent Mixed Brigade. All these formations, except the 49th Division, were also now very much diminished by earlier operations. The 49th Division was Burma Area Army's reserve, of which one regiment was sent to support the 15th Army on the Irrawaddy and the remaining two regiments were deployed behind the 33rd Army on the Burma Road near Maymyo.

The 2nd Division, which had been guarding the coast of south Burma, had been ordered to move to Indo-China where the Japanese had decided to take over complete control from the French colonial government.

Stilwell's forces at this time consisted of the Chinese New 1st Army (30th and 38th Division), the Chinese New 6th Army (14th, 22nd, and 50th Divisions), the British 36th Division, and the "Mars" Task Force (American 475th Infantry and 124th Cavalry Regiments, Chinese 1st Regiment, and American 612th Field Artillery Regiment (Pack)), totalling about 140,000 troops.

On the coast the Japanese 28th Army still had the 54th and 55th Divisions (reinforced by the 72nd Independent Mixed Brigade), whose task was to prevent Christison's XV Corps from advancing over the An and Taungup passes to attack the Japanese communications in the Irrawaddy valley in the rear of the Japanese armies facing north. Opposing these two depleted Japanese divisions were the 25th and 26th Indian Divisions, the 81st and 82nd West African Divisions, and an aggressive and efficient 3rd Commando Brigade, comprising Nos. 1, 5, 42, and 44 Commandos. In all, the forces totalled some 120,000 men. Later an East African brigade was added.

Working conditions for the R.A.F. in Burma were usually difficult, always casual.
▽ Armourers, dressed in typical Burma kit, bring up a rocket for loading onto a Hurricane based on an advanced airstrip in central Burma.
▷ Flight mechanics at work on a Thunderbolt in November 1944.
▷▷ The results of their work: direct hits on road and railway bridges at Monywa on the Chindwin. A detour round the damaged bridge can be clearly seen.

The Allied administrative situation was that the 14th Army could still be supplied as far as the Irrawaddy as long as it was not more than the equivalent of seven divisions totalling 260,000 troops, but after that the numbers must be decreased to a strength of about five divisions. In the latter stages air supply must come from the coastal airfields and not from the Imphal and Agatarla fields. As it happened Akyab was occupied on January 2 and Ramree Island was fully occupied by February 22.

The Allies were again in a dominant position in the air at the beginning of January 1945. They had a first-line strength of 48 fighter and bomber squadrons. These consisted of 17 fighter, 12 fighter-bomber, three fighter-reconnaissance, ten heavy bomber, five medium bomber, and one light bomber squadrons. Together these totalled 4,464 R.A.F. and 186 U.S.A.A.F. aircraft.

Air Command had four troop carrier squadrons and 16 transport squadrons, of which four were R.A.F. and 12 U.S.A.A.F. These were increased to 19 transport squadrons in March and 20 in May, totalling a maximum of 500 transport aircraft. Yet this air transport strength was still insufficient to meet all demands, and the Arakan advance had later to be halted because of the amount of aircraft which had to be diverted to the voracious 14th Army to keep it moving.

Against this air strength the Japanese had a maximum of 66 aircraft, of which only 50 were serviceable by April 1. The Japanese were still using the same type of aircraft as in 1942-3, and their performance could not compare with the modern British and American aircraft of this period.

Command changes

General Stilwell had agreed to serve under the 11th Army Group, but only with the stipulation that when he captured Kamaing he should come under direct command of the Supreme Commander. He had not liked serving under Slim's 14th Army. The result was that Mountbatten had now to deal with two army commanders. In order to regulate this position satisfactorily, Mountbatten asked the Chiefs-of-Staff to appoint a Commander-in-Chief Land Forces South-East Asia who had had experience of having satisfactorily commanded American forces in the field. So,

in November 1944, the 11th Army Group was abolished and a new headquarters Allied Land Forces South-East Asia (A.L.F.S.E.A.) was formed to command all land operations against the Japanese in Burma. This meant the departure of General Giffard, who had been the architect and prime mover of the victories in Burma to this date. Lieutenant-General Sir Oliver Leese, who had commanded 8th Army in Italy, was appointed Commander A.L.F.S.E.A.

Shortly afterwards, Christison's XV Corps, which was mainly concerned in combined operations with the navy along the coast, was taken out of Slim's hands and came directly under the command of Leese, who had had much more experience of seaborne operations. At the same time Slim was relieved of the responsibility of his communications back to India so that he could get on with his tactical land battle without having to worry about administrative problems. It was felt that Slim could best serve the Allies by his undoubted great powers of command and example in the field if he was divorced from administrative work which was not his strong point.

It will be seen from this survey that Slim's 14th Army was at this time only engaging four out of the ten Japanese divisions opposing the Allies, and these four divisions were the weakest the Japanese had in the line, reinforcements to Burma from Japan and elsewhere having ceased in 1944.

Slim's plan was to destroy the Japanese 15th Army between the hammer of Stopford's XXXIII Corps advancing on Mandalay and the armoured anvil of Messervy's IV Corps capturing Meiktila.

This plan depended on the speed and secrecy of Messervy's 150-mile advance west of the Irrawaddy, whilst Stopford held the attention of XV Corps near Mandalay. Rees's 19th Division, to the north of Mandalay, was still the main attraction for the Japanese. Stopford's 20th Division started to cross the Irrawaddy at Myinmu on February 12 at a point about 30 miles downstream from Mandalay. This immediately attracted the Japanese, who counter-attacked the bridgehead repeatedly for the next two weeks.

Stopford's British 2nd Division had to wait for the boats and pontoon rafts used by the 20th Division before they could start to cross on February 21 at Ngazun

◀△ *Tied to a boat, two pack mules swim across the Irrawaddy. The entire train made the 500-yard crossing safely.*
◀▽ *A column of men of the 11th East African Division trudges along the road to Kalewa.*
△ *Casualty Clearing Stations operating just behind the front line were a vital link in the chain of medical care for the wounded. After initial treatment, serious cases were flown out in light aircraft to rear areas. The total army casualties suffered by Britain and her Commonwealth in Burma between 1942 and 1945 were 947 officers killed, 1,837 wounded, and 303 missing, British other ranks 5,037, 10,687, and 2,507; Indian other ranks 8,235, 28,873, and 8,786; African other ranks 858, 3,208, and 200; and Burmese other ranks 249, 129, and 3,052. These give a grand total of 15,326 killed, 44,731 wounded, and 14,852 missing. Including the other services, a total of 31,468 British and Commonwealth men died in the war against Japan – 12.4 per cent of the total British and Commonwealth dead.*

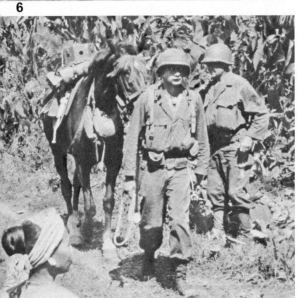

In February 1944 the American 5307th Regiment left Ledo heading into northern Burma. Their aim was to disrupt Japanese communications, travelling through the jungle and living off the land.

1. Casual but tough, two men of the 3rd Battalion take a break.

2. A typical "Merrill's Marauder".

3. After an encounter with the Japanese: removing ammunition from the body of a dead comrade.

4. At Walabum the Marauders fought in conjunction with American and Chinese units of Stilwell's army. For many of them, this was the only occasion when they saw an Allied tank.

5. Emerging from the jungle after two weeks, Marauders meet their first Burmese.

6. Replenishing the water supply. All drinking water was boiled or treated with chlorine tablets in an effort to avoid dysentery.

7. Brigadier-General Frank Merrill, who dreamed up and led the Marauders.

8. Unpacking a parachute container of supplies.

9. There were many such streams to be forded, adding to the difficulties of jungle warfare.

10. Inspecting the enemy after an ambush: note the Marauders' Thompson .45 sub-machine guns.

11. In enemy territory: a well-spaced single column moves with guns at the ready.

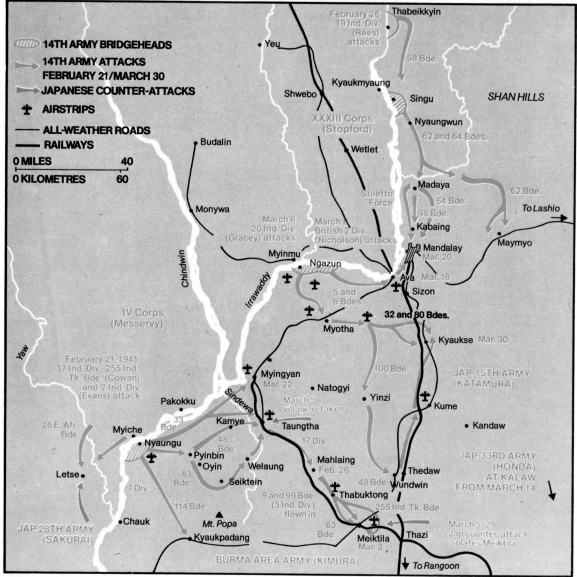

△ Mule-power and man-power bring supplies up from the east bank of the Chindwin, after an unopposed crossing.

▷ △ Men of the 4/4th Royal Garrison Rifles and 2nd Royal Berkshire Regiment move around Fort Dufferin as the 8/12th Frontier Force Regiment prepares to make a frontal attack. The fort was one of the last Japanese strongholds within Mandalay.

▷ On the 36th Division's front near Pinwe, men of a Chinese Heavy Mortar Regiment fuse 4.2-inch mortar bombs before going into action.

▷ ▽ A Priest 105-mm self-propelled howitzer is manned in a hurry.

◁ The battles for Meiktila and Mandalay.

at a point 15 miles from Mandalay. Unfortunately, many of the boats and pontoons had been inadvertently damaged by the 20th Division and the 2nd Division had a difficult crossing. However, these assault crossings achieved the desired strategic effect of attracting the full attention of the tiny Japanese 15th Army, so that when Messervy's 7th Division crossed 90 miles further south on February 13, there was little or no opposition. By the end of February Slim's 14th Army had crossed the 1,000-yard wide swift-flowing Irrawaddy in four places with his northern bridgeheads attracting a violent reaction from the Japanese.

Messervy built up his bridgehead at Nyangu before he made his dash to Meiktila. By February 20 Messervy had got his 17th Division and 255th Tank Brigade across the Irrawaddy into his bridgehead at Nyangu, and was ready to start. Meiktila was 80 miles away across sandy scrub country, broken up by dry river beds. On February 21 Messervy's tanks began to roll. At the same time Major-General G. C. Evans's 7th Division, which had carried out the crossing, was ordered to capture the oil town of Chauk and lead on to Myingyan to the north east. Major-General D. T. Cowan's 17th Division, with its tank brigade, reached the outskirts of Meiktila by the end of February and on March 1, Cowan attacked.

Meiktila fell the following day and its airfield on the eastern edge of the town, which was vital for re-supply and the reinforcement of the defence, was captured on March 3. Cowan did not settle down but immediately sent out fighting patrols of tanks and infantry to seek out and find the enemy.

At this vital juncture Slim flew in with Messervy to visit Cowan and was present to observe a quite severe Japanese counter-attack, in which the British tanks caused many casualties and dispersed the attackers. Two men in the army commander's party were wounded by Japanese artillery fire but Slim, Messervy, and Cowan stood unmoved on the hilltop like Old Testament prophets whilst their men below gained victory.

After a new brigade was flown in Cowan withstood a series of local Japanese counter-attacks. Meanwhile to the north, Stopford, having seen his bridgeheads were secure, made plans for a deliberate advance to capture Mandalay. His plan was that the 19th Division would attack from the north. The 2nd Division would

△ *From their vantage point high on Pagoda Hill, observers look down on the battle raging around Fort Dufferin.*

advance through the old capital of Ava along the Irrawaddy from the west and the 20th Division would sweep round the south to attack Mandalay from the south and the south-east. The 19th Division soon penetrated the town but was held up by defences on Mandalay Hill and the battlements of Fort Dufferin. The 2nd Division was delayed amongst the pagodas of Ava, but the 20th Division made good progress around the south where the opposition was negligible.

As soon as Slim realised that Mandalay was not held in strength, he ordered the 20th Division to send a column south towards Meiktila, leaving the British 2nd Division to surround it from the south.

What was left of the 15th Army in Mandalay was destroyed by heavy bomber attacks. Mandalay became a bomb trap. Meiktila had fallen on March 1 and Mandalay fell on March 20.

At this time the Japanese Intelligence had become completely confused and they did not seem to know what was hitting them and from where. The battles for Meiktila and Mandalay were the death knell of the already depleted 15th Army.

In mid-January the Yunnan Armies at last began to advance across the Salween. Namkham and Wamting were soon captured. By January 18 the American "Mars" Force was overlooking the Mandalay-Lashio road at Hsenwi and was carrying out guerrilla raids along it. On January 21 the Ledo Road to China via Bhamo, Namkham, Muse, and Wamting was opened, followed by the first convoy to China, which arrived at Kunming on February 4.

This date, February 4, 1945, can be said, therefore, to be the date of the completion of the "Quadrant" plan. However, Chiang Kai-shek made this the occasion to start to withdraw his Yunnan armies back into China for the very sensible reason that he wanted now to retake the huge areas of China which the Japanese had recently overrun. This was naturally supported by the Americans, who required these areas for air bases to support their advance towards the invasion of Japan. But some of the more parochial commanders in A.L.F.S.E.A. tended to denigrate the Chinese for marching away from the "battlefields in Burma", perhaps forgetting that the Chinese had been fighting since 1937.

However, Stilwell's forces were still active. By March 1 the Chinese 30th Division had occupied Hsenwi and the British 36th Division was crossing the Shweli at Myitson and Mongmit against the now 3,000-strong 18th Division. The British received 360 casualties during this crossing.

On March 6 the Chinese 38th Division occupied Lashio and by March 24 the Burma Road from Mandalay to Lashio was in Allied hands. The British 36th Division, having captured the ruby mine town of Mogok on March 19, moved to Mandalay when the Northern Combat Area Command ceased to exist.

The American "Mars" Force, the worthy successors of Merrill's Marauders, was moved to China to be dispersed into training cadres to rebuild the Chinese Army along the same lines as Stilwell's Chinese New Armies.

Thus ended the American army involvement in the war in Burma. It can be said with truth that the few representatives of the American army, Merrill's Marauders and "Mars" Force, gave a very good impression by their fighting capabilities and thrustful initiative to their Allies fighting in Burma.

Parts of the Japanese 33rd Army had been moved from the Lashio Road at the end of the Meiktila battle in a vain attempt to save the town. But even with this last-minute reinforcement, the British forces outnumbered their enemy by about ten to one on the ground and about twenty to one in tanks.

IV Corps casualties from the crossing of the Irrawaddy to the end of March were 835 killed, 3,174 wounded, and 90 missing. The high proportion of wounded was because in the Indian Army, anyone who incurred a wound obtained a pension, and so the smallest wounds were noted, whereas in the British units there was no point in worrying about or recording minor wounds. During these battles IV Corps had 26 tanks destroyed and 44 damaged.

XXXIII Corps, in its capture of Mandalay, lost 1,472 killed and 4,933 wounded, with 120 missing. It had one more division than IV Corps and was in action for six weeks before IV Corps had crossed the Irrawaddy, so that the proportion of casualties is comparable.

No. 221 Group (Air Vice-Marshal S. F. Vincent) was in support throughout and flew 4,360 sorties, of which 2,085 were attacks on Japanese positions or their

communications, during which 1,560 tons of bombs were dropped.

The 14th Army was now all set for its dash to capture Rangoon and obtain a port before the monsoon, the opposition to its advance now being negligible.

The final stages

The build-up of Allied naval forces resulted in the command of the Indian Ocean and the Bay of Bengal being regained by the Allies by the beginning of 1945. This made possible not only the more rapid reinforcement of India because troopships were able to sail independently without escort, but amphibious operations could now be undertaken along the

△ ◁ *On the road to Mandalay, January 1945: British troops dig in at the River Mu weir, anticipating a Japanese counter-attack.*
△ *Lieutenant-General Sir William Slim, commander of the 14th Army, stands inside Fort Dufferin.*
▽ *March 1945: the Union Jack flies once more over Fort Dufferin.*

△ *Though the end of the war found the Allies still in Burma, they nevertheless moved swiftly to take the surrender of Japanese troops elsewhere in South-East Asia. These officers from the garrison in Kuala Lumpur, Malaya, are laying down their swords under the terms of the surrender.*
▷△ *A Vultee Vengeance dive-bomber returns to its base, a forward airfield, after a sortie against Japanese positions.*
▷▽ *After an attack by R.A.F. Beaufighters, steam pours from the wrecked engine of a Japanese train in Burma.*

coast of Burma without fear of heavy losses to submarines, and without the need for powerful naval covering forces.

Lieutenant-General Sir Philip Christison was given two tasks to carry out. When the 14th Army crossed the Irrawaddy in February 1945 their supply lines to Assam had become uneconomic. It was therefore necessary to capture airfields along the coast of Arakan, from which the 14th Army could be re-supplied during its advance to Meiktila and south to Rangoon. Without these airfields and the necessary sea ports to land stores, the 14th Army could not advance south. Fortunately the Japanese, as a result of the pressure of the 81st West African Division east of them, had evacuated Akyab on December 31 so that Christison's XV Corps landed unopposed on January 2. He immediately arranged to re-open the port of Akyab for supplies.

The total strength of the British portion of A.L.F.S.E.A. (that is not including the Americans and Chinese) was, by the beginning of 1945, 971,828 men, including 127,139 British troops, 581,548 Indians, 44,988 East Africans, 59,878 West Africans, and 158,275 civilian labourers. Of

these, 260,000 were in the 14th Army, including its line of communications troops.

It was calculated, therefore, that in order to supply the 14th Army as well as XV Corps, whose secondary rôle was to try to contain all Japanese forces (including the 54th Division and remnants of the 55th Division) in the area and to try to prevent their being re-deployed in the Irrawaddy valley, it was necessary to open two new ports. The first was at Akyab, and the second at Kyaukpyu on Ramree Island. From these two ports and from Chittagong the divisions of the 14th Army in central Burma, and the formations of XV Corps operating on the Arakan coast could be maintained if the ports could be built up to a capacity sufficient to handle the necessary sea lift tonnage required.

It was calculated that the port of Akyab would have to maintain 46,000 men, as well as the construction stores required for two all-weather airfields and the tonnage necessary to build up a 20,000-ton reserve for the 14th Army. This would require a maximum sea lift of 850 tons a day in February and March 1945, dropping down to 600 tons in May when the un-

necessary formations of XV Corps, having achieved their object, were sent back to India.

In the same manner it was calculated that the port of Kyaukpyu must maintain 36,000 men from February to May and handle stores sufficient to construct two all-weather airfields and build up a stockpile of 22,000 tons for the 14th Army. The daily sealift required would be 450 tons in February, rising to 650 tons from March to May.

Lieutenant-General M. Kawabe had ordered the 28th Army (Lieutenant-General S. Sakurai) to send its 2nd Division, with a large part of the army's motor transport, to the 33rd Army, which was facing the 14th Army, and to hold with his remaining two divisions (54th and 55th) the Irrawaddy delta and the Arakan coast up to 35 miles north of Kyaukpyu. Later the 2nd Division was to move to Indo-China.

Sakurai was told to hold the offshore islands of Cheduba and Ramree for as long as possible. The removal of the Japanese 2nd Division (on its way to Indo-China), which had previously been responsible for the delta and the remainder of the Burmese coastline further south, meant that Sakurai had to withdraw his 55th Division to protect that area, leaving the 54th Division to face Christison's XV Corps.

Lieutenant-General S. Miyazaki's 54th Division had received orders in December 1944 to protect the rear of the 15th Army in the Irrawaddy valley from any risks of XV Corps cutting their communications between Meiktila and Rangoon. It will be remembered that Miyazaki had carried out the rear guard action of 33rd Division during its wholesale retreat from Kohima brilliantly.

To carry out his orders, Miyazaki had to hold the An and Taungup passes at all costs. As the 81st and then the 82nd West African Division advanced slowly down the Kaladan, Miyazaki decided that he would use a covering force to delay these two divisions for as long as possible whilst basing his main defence in the north at Kangaw, 40 miles east of Akyab. His other strongpoint would be at Taungup itself. Ten miles west of Kangaw lay the Myebon peninsula.

Before Akyab had fallen Christison had already made plans to land on the Myebon peninsula.

XV Corps consisted of the 25th and 26th Indian Divisions, the 81st and 82nd West

African Divisions, and the 3rd Commando Brigade (which was to be increased to four Royal Marine and Army Commandos). Christison now had plenty of landing craft, reinforced with locally constructed craft. Now that the Royal Navy had regained command of the Bay of Bengal and Akyab had fallen, it was possible for XV Corps to advance south. The Myebon peninsula and Ramree Island were held by Japanese outposts covering the main defences on the mainland.

On January 14, the joint force commanders (Rear-Admiral B. C. S. Martin [Flag Officer Force "W"], Lieutenant-General Christison, and Air Vice-Marshal The Earl of Bandon) decided that the 26th Division would assault Ramree on January 21 and the 25th Division (Major-General C. E. N. Lomax) and 3rd Commando Brigade (Brigadier C. R. Hardy) would occupy the Myebon peninsula and strike east towards Kangaw to cut the Japanese 54th Division's communications to the north.

The 3rd Commando Brigade would spearhead the attack on Myebon with the 74th Brigade passing through.

A reconnaissance of the beaches at Myebon by a special boating party found that a line of coconut stakes had been driven in just below the low-water mark about 300 yards offshore. So before the attack, a Combined Operation Piloted Party (part of the special Small Operations Group) went ashore and attached to these stakes explosives timed to go off at zero hour. The anti-boat stakes were thus blown, tearing a gap 25 yards wide for No. 42 (Royal Marine) Commando to land under cover of a smokescreen laid from the air on the morning of January 12.

The Commandos suffered a few casualties from mines on the beach, but quickly formed a beach-head. The landing was supported by the cruiser *Phoebe*, the destroyer *Napier*, the sloops *Narbada* and *Jumna*, and four minesweepers. Forty-nine landing craft of all types (including three L.C.I., five L.C.T., 12 L.C.M., and 18 L.C.A.) landed the commandos.

The Royal Marines found that the beach was too muddy for tanks, vehicles, and stores to land so the Royal Engineers reconnoitred and constructed a new route, using explosives to smooth out a nearby rocky outcrop on which tanks and vehicles could land.

△ ◁ *Improvised gun train in action, carrying a detachment of Rajput gunners escorted by men of the West Yorkshire Regiment.*
▽ ◁ *D.U.K.W.s carry vital supplies down the Chindwin as the 14th Army continues its advance in Burma.*
△ *After the establishment of the bridgeheads over the Irrawaddy, the 19th Division from Singu and the 17th Indian Division from Nyaungu stabbed southward past Meiktila towards the oilfields at Yenangyaung. Most of the damage was caused during the British retreat in 1942.*

△ *Major-General Wynford Rees, commander of the 19th Indian Division.*

▽ *The drive to Rangoon.*

Shortly afterwards No. 5 Commando landed and passed through No. 42 Commando to widen the beach-head.

Nos. 1 and 44 (Royal Marine) Commandos also inadvertently landed on the same beach and pushed ahead. By this time the tanks belonging to the 19th Lancers were ashore.

The Royal Marines of No. 42 Commando occupied Myebon village on the 13th and the village of Kantha was also captured. At this stage the 74th Brigade (Brigadier J. E. Hirst) took up the advance and overcame the remaining opposition and the Commando Brigade was withdrawn to prepare for the Kangaw operation. By the 17th the whole of the Myebon peninsula was captured.

The 82nd West African Division had relieved 81st Division, which was still in the Kaladan valley. The 82nd Division was now commanded by Major-General H. C. Stockwell, who had previously commanded one of the aggressive British 36th Division's two brigades. Advancing south, Stockwell occupied the ancient capital of Arakan, Myohaung, on January 25 and applied pressure on the Japanese facing him. Christison was anxious to cripple the 54th Division by cutting its communications at Kangaw.

The joint force commanders rather over-insured in the force that they used to overcome opposition on Ramree and Cheduba Islands. But at this time of the war it was common policy for the Allies to deploy as much *matériel* strength as possible to save Allied lives if that *matériel* strength could be easily brought to bear without too much delay.

The naval component of this combined operation included the battleship *Queen Elizabeth*, the cruiser *Phoebe*, the destroyers *Rapid* and *Napier*, the Royal Naval sloop *Flamingo*, and the R.I.N. sloop *Kistna*. No. 224 Group supported the attack with its Thunderbolts and Mitchells. Prior to the attack 85 Liberators of the Strategic Air Command bombarded the beaches and its surrounds.

After the naval and air bombardment, the 71st Brigade (Brigadier R. C. Cottrell-Hill), with a squadron of tanks, a regiment of field artillery, and two companies of the Frontier Force machine gun battalion, landed unopposed at 0942 on January 21 west of the town of Kyaukpyu. The leading motor launch and landing craft both struck mines and were blown up, causing some confusion, but the remainder of the landing proceeded without opposition or further delay.

Next day the 4th Brigade (Brigadier J. F. R. Forman) took over the beach-head and the 71st Brigade moved south.

On January 26 the Royal Marine Commandos landed unopposed on the neighbouring Cheduba Island.

By January 31 Lomax had landed the remainder of his 25th Division on Ramree Island. The opposition from the Japanese outposts increased and the Indian brigades, with tanks, slowly and methodically cleared the island until Ramree town itself was occupied on June 9. On this day, under cover of an attack by the remains of the Japanese 5th Air Division, a Japanese destroyer (accompanied by 20 launches) rushed to the rescue of the Japanese and took off over 500 men. By January 17 resistance on the island ended.

The 22nd East African Brigade, which had come under Christison's command, arrived to garrison Ramree and Cheduba Islands so that the 26th Division would be

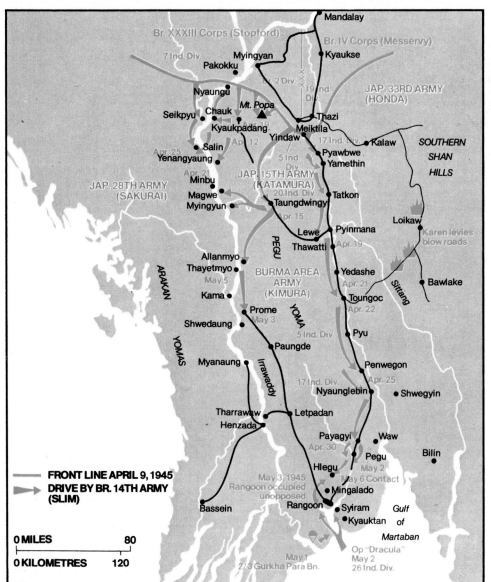

FRONT LINE APRIL 9, 1945
DRIVE BY BR. 14TH ARMY (SLIM)

0 MILES 80
0 KILOMETRES 120

available to land at Toungup.

The fight at Kangaw turned out to be one of the bloodiest and most savage of the Burma campaign. But this fight succeeded in crippling a major part of Miyazaki's 54th Division, which was one of the few divisions in Burma at this time which had not suffered a defeat, was not too depleted, and was still full of fight.

Major-General G. N. Wood's plan for the capture of Kangaw was for the 3rd Commando Brigade (Nos. 1, 5, 42, and 44 Commandos) to seize a bridgehead on the east bank of the Diangbon Chaung two miles south-west of Kangaw. Then his 51st Brigade would pass through the bridgehead and join forces with the 74th Brigade, which was advancing from Kantha across the Min Chaung from the Myebon peninsula. The Japanese would find themselves hemmed in between the two Indian brigades and the West African 82nd Division advancing from the north. Hardy, commanding the 3rd Commando Brigade, wished to go by the indirect route, which he had reconnoitred, and advance up the Diangbon Chaung from

the south and not via the Myebon peninsula, although this meant a trip of 27 miles by boat. On January 21, 50 vessels (including the R.I.N. sloop *Narbada*, a minesweeper, a Landing Craft Tank (carrying a bulldozer and R.E. equipment), four L.C.I.s, 22 L.C.A.s, and some "Z" craft carrying artillery, anchored off the southern entrance of the Diangbon Chaung. The "Z" craft were large but manoeuvrable lighters whose decks had been strengthened with steel so that a troop of 25-pounders could fire from them.

The Diangbon Chaung, as Hardy predicted, had not been mined and the Japanese did not see the approach of the attack. The Royal Navy and R.I.N. bombarded the beaches, supported by the medium bombers of No. 224 Group, which also laid a smokescreen. Surprise was complete and No. 1 Commando pushed on to Hill 170 which was to be the scene of heavy fighting. By nightfall No. 5 Commando had landed, with the next day Nos. 44 (R.M.) and 42 (R.M.) Commandos.

The Japanese on the spot counter-attacked fiercely and efforts to infiltrate

▽ *Patching a damaged bridge with a "scissors" section. Carried on a turretless Covenanter or Valentine tank, this "Scissors Bridge, 30-foot, No. 1" could span a gap of 30 feet and bear a weight of up to 30 tons. They were widely used in the North-West European and Mediterranean theatres, and were particularly useful in Burma, where they made a real contribution to the 14th Army's swift advance.*

△ *Pathans of the Punjab Regiment move against Japanese positions during the 19th Indian Division's drive forward on March 1.*
▷ *Some of the thousands of Japanese who died during their tenacious, bitterly-fought defence in Burma.*
▷▷ *A wounded prisoner escorted by two of his Indian captors.*

the village of Kangaw were rebuffed. The Japanese heavily bombarded the beaches with field artillery on the 24th and 25th, but on the 26th the 51st Brigade (Brigadier R. A. Hutton) landed with a troop of medium tanks followed by the 53rd Brigade (Brigadier B. C. H. Gerty).

As soon as he heard of the landing, General Miyazaki ordered Major-General T. Koba, commanding the "Matsu" Detachment, to repel the invaders and keep open the road. Koba, as a colonel, had commanded the two battalion column which had so successfully driven the 81st West African Division out of the Kaladan in March 1944. The "Matsu" Detachment consisted of the 54th Infantry Group, comprising three infantry battalions and an artillery battalion. Koba arrived on January 31 and immediately launched a heavy attack on Hill 170, which was held by Nos. 1 and 42 Royal Marine Commandos, commanded by Colonel Peter Young, Hardy's second in command.

The Commandos, supported by three tanks, repulsed Koga's most determined assaults. Attack and counter-attack waged around Hill 170 for 36 hours. The "Matsu" Detachment finally launched a pole-charge tank hunting party of en-gineers. They destroyed two tanks and damaged the third with a loss of 70 of their own men killed. By this time the 74th Brigade was moving in from the north-west: but not before the Commandos had killed over 300 Japanese at a loss to themselves of 66 killed, 15 missing, and 259 wounded. Lieutenant Knowland, of No. 1 Commando, won a posthumous Victoria Cross for his part in the fighting.

As soon as Miyazaki heard that Ramree Island had been occupied he feared that the 26th Division might land in his rear, so he ordered the "Matsu" Detachment to break off the engagement and withdraw to the An Pass, which was vital to the 54th Division's communications. By February 18, the 25th Indian Division had relieved the Commando brigade.

Miyazaki had received heavy casualties but had skillfully avoided the destruction of his force.

It will be remembered that during February IV Corps and XXXIII Corps had crossed the Irrawaddy and by March 1 Meiktila had fallen. Also at this time the Chinese were asking for an air lift of their forces in Burma to take part in the offensive to regain the two provinces that they had lost a few months previously. Transport aircraft, therefore, were at a premium and S.E.A.C. decided that air supply to XV Corps must cease.

Lieutenant-General Sir Oliver Leese (C.-in-C. A.L.F.S.E.A.) therefore decided to withdraw the 25th and 26th Divisions to India. The 26th Division was withdrawn to prepare for a landing at Rangoon. The Commandos had already been withdrawn to train for a landing on the coast of Malaya.

It is an opportune time to consider the effects of the Arakan campaign. Strangely enough, both sides achieved their main objects. The Japanese, with their depleted forces, prevented XV Corps from breaking into the Irrawaddy valley although this was never XV Corps' intention. On the other hand XV Corps captured Akyab without a shot being fired and Ramree Island with trifling loss, although again the Japanese never had any intention of defending them strongly. Without doubt Miyazaki had done very well against the equivalent of five divisions (25th and 26th Indian, 81st and 82nd West African, and 22nd East African Brigade and 3rd Commando Brigade), supported by overwhelming numbers of aircraft and naval ships. As so often occurred in this campaign, XV Corps' main enemy was geography and

the problem of how to apply their superior forces effectively against a skilful enemy in difficult terrain. However, it is now known that Christison had a greater success than he first realised. Only four battalions of both the Japanese 54th and 55th Divisions arrived in time to assist the 33rd Army in its operations against 14th Army. The result was that the 14th Army had nothing but the remains of divisions which had already been virtually destroyed to oppose it in its advance south.

During these operations XV Corps lost 5,089 casualties, of which 1,138 were killed. No. 224 Group (The Earl of Bandon) lost 78 aircraft, but claimed 63 Japanese aircraft destroyed. Fortunately there had never been any serious opposition to the seaborne landings, but during them the Royal Navy fired 23,000 rounds varying from 4-inch to 15-inch calibre. The Navy had landed in all 54,000 men, 800 animals, 11,000 vehicles, and 14,000 tons of stores.

The final seaborne operation of the Burma war was the assault on Rangoon, which started with an airborne attack on Elephant Point, which covered the entrance of the main navigable arm of the Irrawaddy river leading from the sea to Rangoon itself. The amphibious operation

for the capture of Rangoon was launched on April 27, while the 14th Army was held up at Prome and the Pegu river.

Two naval forces set sail to give long range protection to the large convoy during its voyage to the mouth of the Rangoon river and to intercept any fleeing Japanese.

The first, under Vice-Admiral Walker, was directed against the Andaman and Nicobar Islands, covering Rangoon from the west. It consisted of the battleships *Queen Elizabeth* and *Richelieu*, the cruisers *Cumberland, Suffolk, Ceylon*, and *Tromp*, the escort carriers *Empress* and *Shah*, six destroyers, and two resupply oil tankers. On the morning of April 30, Walker bombarded targets in the Nicobars and in the evening put in airstrikes and naval bombardments on to airfields, docks, and shipping at Port Blair in the Andamans. Before leaving the area on May 7, Walker also attacked Victoria Point and Mergui near to the Malay border and returned for a second strike at Port Blair and the Nicobars.

The second naval force consisted of three destroyers under Commodore A. L. Poland. On the night of April 29-30 Poland intercepted a convoy of small ships carrying about 1,000 men and stores from Rangoon to Moulmein. He sank ten craft and picked up some survivors.

At 0230 hours on May 1 a visual control post was dropped as a marker for a parachute landing. Thirty-eight Dakotas dropped a composite battalion of the 50th Gurkha Parachute Brigade at 0545 hours. There were five minor casualties. A further 32 casualties were caused amongst the Gurkhas when some Liberators, aiming at another target, dropped a stick of bombs on the paratroopers. The Gurkhas overcame a small force of 37 Japanese holding Elephant Point itself. The way was then clear for landing craft carrying the assault troops to advance up the river as soon as any mines had been swept.

Aircraft flying over Rangoon saw the words "Japs gone" and "Extract Digit" painted on the roof of Rangoon Jail. Wing-Commander A. E. Saunders (commanding No. 110 Squadron R.A.F.), seeing this well known R.A.F. slang and seeing no signs of the enemy, landed at Mingaladon Airfield, but unfortunately damaged his Mosquito in the craters on the runway. Saunders, having contacted the British prisoners-of-war in Rangoon Jail and hearing that the Japanese had evacuated Rangoon on April 29, went down to the docks and sailed down the Rangoon River in a motor launch to report that the Japanese had gone. Meanwhile, the brigades of the 26th Division moved up the Rangoon river in landing craft and soon occupied Rangoon. It was a tragedy that Colonel Dick Ward, who had been Commander Royal Engineers of the 17th Indian Division from its retreat from Moulmein in 1942 to India and had fought throughout the campaign, was killed when the landing craft in which he was travelling in the van to occupy Rangoon on May 2, 1945 struck a mine.

The battles for Mandalay and Meiktila were over. The Japanese 15th Army which had attacked Kohima/Imphal, and the 33rd Army had both suffered a major defeat. The 33rd Army had been severely mauled by the Chinese and Stilwell's N.C.A.C. (including the British 36th Division). During their counter-attack to recapture Meiktila, their losses were again heavy. The 18th Division also had suffered 1,773 casualties, which was about one-third of its strength and lost about half of their 45 guns. The 49th Division, which (being fairly new in Burma) started with a total strength of 10,000, suffered 6,500 casualties and lost all but three of its 48

guns. Casualties amongst the other divisions were of a similar order. As the official British history states of this period, the Burma Area Army had virtually ceased to exist as a fighting force. Already, by August 1944, the Southern Army had been told that it could expect no further reinforcements in men or *matériel* from Japan, and the divisions were now living on their own fat.

The 28th Army, which was mainly concerned with defending the coast of Burma, had a small force (72nd Independent Mixed Brigade) in the Mount Popa-Chauk-Yenangyaung area but, as related, only four battalions of the 54th and 55th Divisions facing XV Corps were ever deployed in Central Burma to oppose the 14th Army.

General Leese had ordered Slim to reduce the strength of his army to four and two-thirds divisions, which was the maximum number which could be supplied by air during his drive south. XXXIII Corps (Stopford) was to advance down the Irrawaddy valley from Yenanyaung, via Magwe and Allanmyo to the railhead at Prome and on towards Rangoon if it had not already been captured. IV Corps (Messervy) was to use the main road route to Rangoon via Pyabwe, Pyinmana, Toungoo, and Pegu. Each corps would consist of two motorised infantry divisions and one armoured brigade.

The plan was that each corps would move in bounds one division at a time passing through the other, from airfield to airfield, supplied by air-landed stores at each point. Travelling with the divisions would be a large number of airfield construction engineers. As the left flank of Messerby's IV Corps would be in the air, Mountbatten decided to organise the loyal Karens in the hills flanking his advance into levies to protect his eastern flank. Over 3,000 of these fine guerrilla fighters were recruited, and Messervy had then no reason to worry about any unexpected attack from that direction as the Karens were only too glad of the chance to kill Japanese.

Each corps had a distance of 350 miles to go to its objective. XXXIII Corps consisted of the 7th and 20th Indian Divisions and the 268th Indian Infantry Brigade, plus the 254th Indian Tank Brigade. IV Corps consisted of the 5th and 17th Indian Divisions and the 255th Indian Tank Brigade. Each corps had its own artillery component which included two medium regiments with XXXIII Corps

Whilst the paucity of the proportion of casualties suffered by the Indian and, to a lesser extent, the British Armies in Burma, bears out the American viewpoint that Britain was not interested in the war and was not prepared to fight, a major factor in the apparent listlessness, lassitude, and absence of offensive spirit in the British Commonwealth forces was disease, which destroyed beyond recovery a large portion of the armed forces each year.

It is a fact that while the Japanese were stationed in areas of fairly low malarial intensity, and amongst a small, hygiene-minded rural population, the British forces were compelled by circumstances to operate in areas of hyperendemic malarial intensity, backing onto disease-ridden urban areas of poverty, overpopulation, and abysmal hygiene standards.

The remarkable improvement in disease statistics once the British forces entered and remained in the comparatively hygienic areas of Burma in 1945 fully illustrates this point.

Admissions into hospitals in the S.E.A.C. area (per 1,000 men) were 885 in 1942, 1,151 in 1943, 993 in 1944, and 462 in 1945 (for all diseases to all troops); 877, 1,073, 911, and 466 (for all diseases to Indian troops only); 460 (52%), 590 (51%), 544 (59%), and 372 (81%) (malaria to all troops, with this as a percentage of all disease admissions); 35.6, 45.5, 47.9, and 49.9 (injuries to all troops not as a result of enemy action); and 6.2, 8.4, 47.4, and 38.9 (injuries to all troops as a result of enemy action). This shows clearly that even during the critical battles of 1944, hospital admissions for malaria were 20 times as great as those for battle casualties.

2965

and one medium regiment with IV Corps. There was a special headquarters Royal Engineer Regiment to control the forward airfield engineers and bridging companies with each corps.

A brigade from the 19th Indian Division accompanied IV Corps and garrisoned its communications as it advanced.

Stopford was held up at Pyabwe by the fine defence of the remnants of the famous 18th Division (now only 2,000 strong) which had captured Singapore, had been one of the first divisions to conquer Burma, and had fought for so long on the northern front against Stilwell.

Otherwise there were no hitches except those caused by geography and the weather. Messervy reached Pyinmana on April 19, Toungoo on the 22nd, and Pegu, within 50 miles of Rangoon, on May 1. At Pegu a Japanese improvised brigade, made up of training unit personnel and numbering 1,700 men, delayed his advance. Unseasonable heavy rain on May 2 stopped IV Corps' advance abruptly. However, the engineers managed to clear

500 mines and to throw a bridge across the Pegu river and at 0930 hours on May 4, IV Corps continued its advance. On May 6 the 1/7th Gurkhas, crossing a blown-up bridge at Hlegu, met a column of the Lincolnshire Regiment from the 26th Division, which had advanced northwards from Rangoon.

Meanwhile XXXIII Corps advanced down the Irrawaddy valley. Stopford captured Chauk on April 18 and Magwe and Yenangyaung on April 21, overcoming resistance from the 72nd Independent Mixed Brigade and some battalions from the 28th Army. Allanmyo on the Irrawaddy was captured on April 28 and Stopford entered Prome on May 3. A patrol from XV Corps, advancing from Taungup, contacted him shortly afterwards so that by that date all three corps of Leese's forces were in touch.

On June 1, 1945, a 12th Army was formed under command of General Stopford to control all operations in Burma, including the maintenance of internal security and the re-establishment of civil government. The 12th Army consisted of IV Corps in the Sittaung valley and the 7th and 20th Indian Divisions and the 268th Brigade in the Irrawaddy valley.

IV Corps consisted of the 5th, 17th, and 19th Indian Divisions, and the 255th Tank Brigade. So with the 7th and 20th Indian Divisions and 268th Brigade, Stopford had five divisions and two brigades under command, with the 26th Division awaiting transport for India. His air support was provided by No. 221 Group R.A.F., but now that the monsoon had broken and flying conditions and visibility was bad, the R.A.F. was not in a position to give good close support to the troops on the ground. Slim, now promoted General, had moved back to Delhi in India to replace Leese.

Stopford's main problem was the Japanese 28th Army which still totalled nearly 30,000 troops, including a multitude of small administrative units.

Sakurai, the army commander, had managed to get the remains of his 54th and 55th Divisions back from the coast and delta over the Irrawaddy and into the Pegu Yomas, a series of jungle-covered hills lying between the Irrawaddy valley on the one hand and the Sittang valley on the other, north of Rangoon. Sakurai's object was to break out and join the remains of the Burma Area Army, which was now regrouping east of the wide flowing and flooded Sittang River. At this time the Sittang was flooded as far north

As their army's organisation disintegrated and their morale crumbled, more and more Japanese soldiers decided it was better to surrender to the enemy than die fighting for the Emperor.
◄ *The first organised party of Japanese to surrender. Men of the 53rd Infantry Division crossed the Sittang river in landing craft to surrender to the 1/10th Gurkhas – who chose the spot where, in 1942, their own division had been defeated by the Japanese.*
◄▽ *Prisoners being brought in for interrogation.*
▽ *Men of the Royal Garhwal Rifles, 26th Indian Division, searching a group of Japanese after the surrender in Malaya.*

△ *S.E.A.C. chiefs draw up the surrender terms. From left to right: Slim, Wheeler, Mountbatten, Power, Park, Browning.*
▷ *Walking from their aircraft to meet their Allied victors – Lieutenant-General Takazo Numato (with glasses) and Rear-Admiral Keigye Chudo.*
▽ *The formal act of surrender took place in the throne room of Government House, Rangoon.*

as Shwegyin, a distance of nearly 50 miles upstream from the Gulf of Martaban. Sakurai decided therefore to advance on a wide 100-mile front between Toungoo and Nyaunglebin, just west of Shwegyin.

It would be tedious here to attempt to describe the numerous small operations which occurred as Sakurai's 28th Army attempted to cross the road in dispersal groups during May and August, all the while being hunted by Stopford's Indian battalions, tanks, and armoured cars. These operations were carried out mainly by junior officers and it was very important to them.

However, a brief resumé of the casualties incurred at that time will indicate the intensity of the fighting and the miserable defeat of the remnants of a once fine army.

On June 28, 1945 the strength of the 28th Army was stated to be 27,764. Three months later, on September 22, the 28th Army's reported strength to the Burma Area Army was as follows: present on duty 7,949; in hospital 1,919; and missing 3,822, some of whom were expected to return.

IV Corps' losses over much the same period were 435 killed, 1,452 wounded, and 42 missing.

Thus in effect ended the war in Burma, where an army of ten Japanese divisions, two Independent Mixed Brigades, and about two Indian National Army divisions were not only defeated, but to all intents and purposes, wiped out as a fighting force.

CHAPTER 176
The last invasion?

by Jenny Shaw

◁ *General Douglas MacArthur, commander designate of the U.S. forces for the invasion of the Japanese home islands.*
▽ *Grenade practice for U.S. Army infantry. It was to be expected that the Japanese would defend their motherland with more than normal tenacity, and the Americans placed great reliance on their superiority in weapons to overcome their more numerous opponents.*

The defeat of Germany took precedence over that of Japan, but within the limits that this imposed, the overall Allied strategy with regard to Japan was to advance by way of the central and southwest Pacific to recapture the Philippines or Formosa with the objective of eventually blockading and possibly invading Japan herself.

When American forces captured the Marianas in June 1944, they breached Japan's inner defence perimeter and brought the Japanese home-land within striking distance of long-range bomber aircraft. At this time too, the greater part of Japan's naval air arm was destroyed in the Battle of the Philippine Sea.

On October 3, 1944, the American Chiefs-of-Staff decided on the strategy to be adopted for the remainder of 1944 and for the following year. MacArthur was ordered to invade Luzon, and Nimitz was to capture one island in the Bonins and one in the Ryūkyūs, the latter for development into an advanced naval and air base for the invasion of Japan contemplated for the autumn of 1945.

Germany surrendered at the beginning of May 1945, and the American Chiefs-of-Staff turned their attention to ending the war against Japan as quickly as possible. With the end of resistance on Okinawa in June 1945, the American forces were in an even better position to blockade Japan, thus cutting her off from the Asian mainland, and to step up their bombing of Japanese cities and so bring the economic life of Japan to a halt. They were also in a

good position to invade Japan if this was considered necessary.

General Curtis LeMay, of the 21st Bomber Command, thought that the war could be ended without invading Japan. He was convinced that with an adequate supply of aircraft and bombs, air power on its own could bring about the Japanese surrender. His own command was due to be enlarged by reinforcements from Europe and India, and he therefore saw no difficulty in stepping up the weight of his offensive after April 1945. LeMay based his assumptions on the results of the five incendiary attacks on Japan in March 1945, and his programme for the defeat of Japan comprised attacks on aircraft factories, industrial cities, oil refineries, storage plants, and in addition, mine-laying to prevent the import to Japan of food and raw materials from Manchuria, Korea, and China.

The American Joint Chiefs, however, did not think that unconditional surrender could be obtained without a successful invasion of Japan. They saw the close sea blockade of Japan and the intensive bombing offensives from Okinawa, Iwo Jima, and the Marianas as preliminaries to the invasion attempt itself. By these means, Japan's industry and communications, and her people's will to resist, would all be considerably weakened.

On April 3, 1945, the Joint Chiefs instructed General Douglas MacArthur (who would lead the invasion) to begin drawing up the plans for the invasion of

◄◄ Vice-Admiral Jessie B. Oldendorf, commander of the special strike force, consisting of the large cruisers Alaska *and* Guam, *set up on July 1, 1945 to make fast surface sweeps through Japanese waters in search of surface shipping.*
◄ Rear-Admiral Clifton A. F. Sprague, who had distinguished himself in the Battle off Samar, and continued in command of escort-carrier groups for the rest of the war.

southern Kyūshū in November 1945 to secure forward sea and air bases for the main invasion effort to take place on the Tokyo plain of Honshū in March 1946.

In readiness for the invasion, the command structure in the Pacific was reorganised. MacArthur was given command of all Army forces and resources, while Admiral Nimitz was to be naval commander. On July 10, a third command, the U.S. Army Strategic Air Force for the Pacific, under General Spaatz, was established to control the air forces involved in the invasion. There was to be no supreme commander in the Pacific, and much was to depend on the ability of MacArthur, Nimitz, and Spaatz to cooperate closely together.

MacArthur's and Nimitz's staffs worked on the plans, and on May 25, MacArthur and Nimitz were officially ordered to undertake the invasion of Kyūshū (Operation "Olympic") on November 1, 1945, and of Honshū (Operation "Coronet") on March 1, 1946. When the Japanese capitulated in August 1945, planning for the invasion had reached an advanced stage.

Prior to the invasion, the Strategic Air Force, based on the Marianas and on Okinawa, would continue its offensive against Japanese industrial centres and lines of communication. To aid this programme, Okinawa and Ie shima were to be developed into a massive air base for some 240 squadrons.

Meanwhile, the Fast Carrier Force would make repeated attacks to destroy Japanese naval and air forces and disrupt land and sea communications.

The Far East Air Force was to neutralise the Japanese air forces in Japan itself and stationed on the Asiatic mainland, harass shipping routes between Asia and Japan, and destroy communications on Kyūshū along with defence installations there.

Operation "Olympic"

Operation "Olympic" had to be undertaken with troops at hand. The bulk of the forces for the invasion of Japan were to be American, although three divisions from the Commonwealth – one from Britain, one from Canada, and one from Australia – were earmarked for later in the Honshū campaign. A small number of Commonwealth air squadrons would participate, in addition to the British Pacific Fleet.

The U.S. 6th Army, comprising some 500,000 men and commanded by General Walter Krueger, was chosen for the initial assault.

Before the actual invasion, a preliminary operation was to be carried out to occupy the islands lying to the west and south of Kyūshū, so that air raid warning facilities, advanced naval anchorages, and sea-plane bases could be established before the landings on Kyūshū.

Three corps, each comprising three divisions, were to land on southern Kyūshū

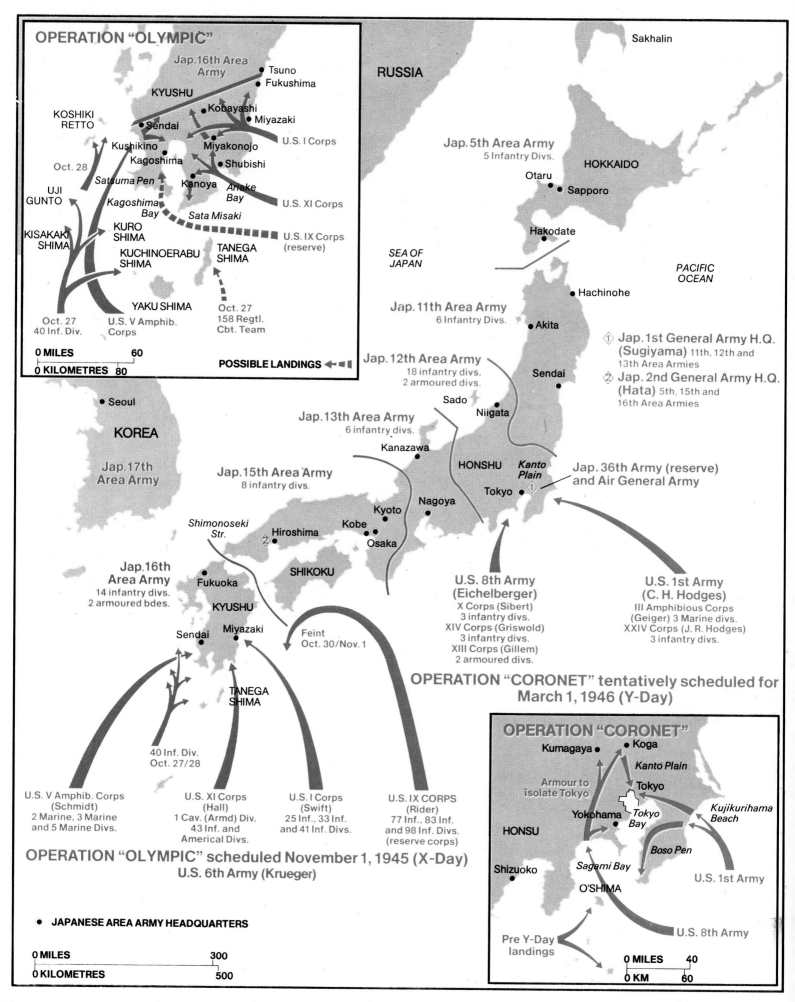

OPERATION "OLYMPIC"

Jap. 16th Area Army

KYUSHU

Tsuno
Fukushima
Kobayashi
Miyazaki
Sendai
Kushikino
Miyakonojo
Kagoshima
Shubishi
Kanoya
Ariake Bay
Satsuma Pen
Kagoshima Bay
Sata Misaki

KOSHIKI RETTO

Oct. 28

UJI GUNTO

KISAKAKI SHIMA

KURO SHIMA

KUCHINOERABU SHIMA

TANEGA SHIMA

YAKU SHIMA

Oct. 27
40 Inf. Div.

U.S. V Amphib. Corps

Oct. 27
158 Regtl. Cbt. Team

U.S. I Corps

U.S. XI Corps

U.S. IX Corps (reserve)

POSSIBLE LANDINGS

| 0 MILES | 60 |
| 0 KILOMETRES | 80 |

RUSSIA

Sakhalin

Jap. 5th Area Army
5 Infantry Divs.

HOKKAIDO

Otaru
Sapporo

Hakodate

SEA OF JAPAN

PACIFIC OCEAN

Hachinohe

Jap. 11th Area Army
6 Infantry Divs.

Akita

Jap. 12th Area Army
18 infantry divs,
2 armoured divs.

Sado

Sendai

Niigata

① Jap. 1st General Army H.Q.
(Sugiyama) 11th, 12th and
13th Area Armies

② Jap. 2nd General Army H.Q.
(Hata) 5th, 15th and
16th Area Armies

Jap. 13th Area Army
6 infantry divs.

Kanazawa

HONSHU

Kanto Plain

Seoul

KOREA

Jap. 17th Area Army

Jap. 15th Area Army
8 infantry divs.

Tokyo ①

Jap. 36th Army (reserve)
and Air General Army

Shimonoseki Str.

Hiroshima ②

Kobe
Kyoto
Nagoya
Osaka

SHIKOKU

Jap. 16th Area Army
14 infantry divs.
2 armoured bdes.

Fukuoka

KYUSHU

Sendai
Miyazaki

Feint
Oct. 30/Nov. 1

U.S. 8th Army
(Eichelberger)
X Corps (Sibert)
3 infantry divs.
XIV Corps (Griswold)
3 infantry divs.
XIII Corps (Gillem)
2 armoured divs.

U.S. 1st Army
(C. H. Hodges)
III Amphibious Corps
(Geiger) 3 Marine divs.
XXIV Corps (J. R. Hodges)
3 infantry divs.

TANEGA SHIMA

40 Inf. Div.
Oct. 27/28

OPERATION "CORONET" tentatively scheduled for
March 1, 1946 (Y-Day)

U.S. V Amphib. Corps
(Schmidt)
2 Marine, 3 Marine
and 5 Marine Divs.

U.S. XI Corps
(Hall)
1 Cav. (Armd) Div.
43 Inf. and
American Divs.

U.S. I Corps
(Swift)
25 Inf., 33 Inf.
and 41 Inf. Divs.

U.S. IX CORPS
(Rider)
77 Inf., 83 Inf.
and 98 Inf. Divs.
(reserve corps)

OPERATION "OLYMPIC" scheduled November 1, 1945 (X-Day)
U.S. 6th Army (Krueger)

● **JAPANESE AREA ARMY HEADQUARTERS**

| 0 MILES | 300 |
| 0 KILOMETRES | 500 |

OPERATION "CORONET"

Kumagaya
Koga
Kanto Plain
Tokyo
Armour to isolate Tokyo
Yokohama
Tokyo Bay
Kujikurihama Beach
HONSU
Boso Pen
Shizuoko
Sagami Bay
O'SHIMA
U.S. 1st Army
U.S. 8th Army
Pre Y-Day landings

| 0 MILES | 40 |
| 0 KM | 60 |

and establish bridgeheads. I Corps would land in the Miya-zaki area, XI Corps in Ariake wan (bay), and V Amphibious Corps in the bay to the south of Kushi-kino. Air attacks were planned to prevent the Japanese bringing up reinforcements to the battle area from the north by road or along the coasts. Within the bridge-heads, work was to begin straightaway on the construction of airfields and bases. Following this, additional areas were to be seized for airfields.

The prime objective of Operation "Olympic" was Kagoshima wan, a 50-mile bay which was to be opened up to Allied shipping and through which would flow most of the men and supplies for the Honshū invasion build-up. Kagoshima wan was also to serve as the navy's advance base.

No advance beyond this would be made, the object of "Olympic" being to secure bases for Operation "Coronet".

If the 14 divisions allotted to the 6th U.S. Army were unable to capture and hold southern Kyūshū, they could be reinforced from December by three divisions per month, intended for Honshū.

The Navy's task in Operation "Olympic" would be to bring reinforcements and supplies to the 6th Army, to cover and support land operations in Kyūshū, to establish a forward base at Kagoshima wan, and to hold island positions necessary for the security of lines of communication.

For Operation "Olympic", Admiral Nimitz divided the American fleet into two—the 3rd and the 5th fleets. The 3rd Fleet, under Admiral William F. Halsey, consisted of a number of fast carrier groups plus supporting battleships, cruisers, and destroyers. Its two main components were Vice-Admiral John Towers's 2nd Carrier Task Force (T.F. 38) and Vice-Admiral H. Bernard Rawlings's British Carrier Task Force (T.F. 37). The 3rd Fleet was to operate against the Kuriles, Hokkaido, and Honshū.

The 5th Fleet, commanded by Admiral Raymond A. Spruance, contained 2,902 vessels, and its main components were the 1st Fast Carrier Force under Vice-Admiral F. C. Sherman (T.F. 58), the Amphibious Force under Admiral Richmond Kelly Turner (T.F. 40), which would land the troops, the Gunfire and Covering Force (T.F. 54) for bombardment and fire support, and T.F. 56, responsible for mine-sweeping operations. The naval bombardment was to begin eight days before the

invasion, and continue until after the launching of the assault.

These were the plans which existed for Operation "Olympic". The second stage of the conquest of the Japanese home islands, Operation "Coronet"—the invasion of Honshū—was scheduled for March 1, 1946.

◄◄ *American plans for the seaborne assault on Japan. If the invasion had been launched, it would have been the largest amphibious attack of all time.*
△△ *and △ Japanese civilians under training. In the event of an invasion, Imperial General Headquarters planned to call up most of the male population, arming them with bamboo spears.*

Operation "Coronet"

According to the plans that had been drawn up, the troops were to be landed on the Kanto plain, east of Tokyo, a level area with good beaches, which would benefit Allied superiority in armour and

▷ *The Japanese heavy cruiser* Tone *(eight 8-inch guns) under air attack in Kure harbour. She was sunk in this raid of July 24, 1945, by aircraft of Task Force 38. In strikes by Task Force 38 on this date and on the 28th, three battleships (*Haruna, Ise, *and* Hyuga*), two heavy cruisers (*Tone *and* Aoba*), and two obsolete cruisers were sunk. The light cruiser* Kitagami, *five destroyers, and many other craft were heavily damaged, and the new carrier* Amagi *was set on fire and later capsized. The carriers* Katsuragi *and* Ryuho *were also put out of action. By the end of the war, virtually all the major units of the Japanese Navy had been lost.*

△▷ *and* ▷▷ *American assault troops in training. No matter how high a standard this reached, however, the men of the 6th, and later the 1st and 8th, Armies had the prospect of very heavy casualties ahead of them.*

mechanisation, and good harbours for the logistic support of the operation. The centre of Japanese political and industrial life was sited in this region, and the American planners felt certain that a defeat here would firmly convince the Japanese that the war was lost.

Only the general outlines of the plan for Operation "Coronet" were fixed when the Japanese capitulated. The final details had still to be settled. However, it is clear that two American armies under MacArthur's command were to take part – the U.S. 1st Army commanded by General Courtney H. Hodges, and comprising XXIV Corps (Lieutenant-General J. R. Hodge) and III Amphibious Corps (Major-General Roy Geiger); and the U.S. 8th Army under General R. L. Eichelberger, comprising X Corps (Major-General F. C. Sibert), XIV Corps (Major-General Oscar Griswold), and XIII Corps (Major-General Alvan Gillem jnr.).

Air support was expected to come from 40 air groups based on Kyūshū, and from a similar force from fields in Iwo Jima, the Marianas, and the Ryūkyūs.

General Eichelberger's 8th Army was to land in Sagami bay and strike north and east to clear the western shore of Tokyo bay as far north as Yokohama. Armoured forces would simultaneously drive north to cut off any Japanese reinforcements. Some of the armour would then be available to assist the 1st Army in the capture of Tokyo, should this prove necessary. At the same time, other divisions would be used to capture Yokohama.

In April 1945, Imperial General Headquarters of Japan concluded that Ameri-

can forces, already stationed in the Bonins and the Ryūkyūs, were quite likely to invade Kyūshū with between 15 and 20 divisions in October 1945, and then to invade Honshū in March 1946 with up to 30 divisions. They expected the Americans to intensify incendiary bombing attacks and the close blockade in the summer months, and then to concentrate on the destruction of the Japanese air forces. Consequently they decided it would be expedient to decentralise control.

Imperial General H.Q. formulated a plan for the defence of Japan, namely "KETSU-GO", which divided Japan's home islands, plus Korea, into seven zones, which were all designated certain army areas. The most likely invasion areas, Kyūshū (16th Area Army) and Tokyo (12th Area Army) were allotted 65 infantry divisions, two armoured divisions, 25 independent mixed brigades, three guards brigades, and seven tank brigades – in all, well over half the total of forces available. Arrangements were made for one area to reinforce another if necessary, although it was realised that the individual islands might well be isolated from each other. Continuous defences were to be constructed on the probable landing sites, but out of reach of American naval bombardment. It was hoped that coastal defence divisions would contain the invaders in their beach-head, and that mobile assault divisions would then move up and eliminate the enemy.

Plans were made for the unification of all communications under control of the Transportation and Communications Ministry, although the Army was to take

over the railways in event of invasion.

The plan emphasised the need for the government, the people, and the armed forces to be completely united and for the entire nation to be armed and ready to fight for the homeland. Where few regular troops were stationed, guerrilla forces were to be organised and trained.

On April 8, 1945, Air General Army Headquarters were established under General M. Kawabe, to control air defences. Its tasks were to attempt to hamper the Americans' invasion preparations, to counter American air attacks on Japan, Korea, and the China coast, and also to build up the strength of the air force to counter losses already sustained.

General Kawabe formed a number of special *kamikaze* units, as he felt these would be the most effective arm against the invaders. These units were dispersed to secret air bases throughout Japan. Obsolete aircraft were converted to *kamikaze* craft. By the end of June, Kawabe hoped to have 2,000 *kamikazes*, and a further 1,000 by August.

To meet the invasion, it was estimated that, by August, Air General Army would have 800 fighter and bomber aircraft in addition to the *kamikazes*, and approximately 13 million gallons of fuel.

With regard to the navy, there were merely 19 destroyers (with only 3,500 tons of fuel for each one) and 38 submarines to repel the invasion. The destroyers were to be kept in the Inland Sea and used within 180 miles of Kyūshū and Shikoku, and the largest of the submarines were to attack the American advanced naval bases at Ulithi, Leyte, and Okinawa. Medium-sized submarines were to attack convoys on supply routes to the north while the small submarine craft patrolled home waters.

There was also a secondary fleet which, by July 1945, consisted of 3,294 vessels of various types including suicide boats, midget submarines, and human torpedoes. This fleet was organised into eight squadrons, and in deploying these, priority was given firstly to Kyūshū, secondly to the Shikoku coastal area, and finally to the Tokyo coastal area.

The naval air forces had the task of crushing any invasion force whilst it was still at sea. By August 1, 1946, it was estimated that the naval air arm would have approximately 5,145 aircraft. But there would be only two million gallons of fuel, however. Agreements defining the Army and Navy areas of responsibility

were drawn up in April, but the proposals were never enacted.

On June 6, 1945, the Chiefs of the Armed Services laid before Japan's Supreme Council a memorandum entitled *The Fundamental Policy to be followed henceforth in the Conduct of the War*, calling for mass mobilisation. To support their proposed policy, they also submitted two subsidiary papers, *Estimates of the World Situation* and *The Present State of National Power*, and these gave no grounds for confidence that the fundamental policy outlined would succeed. The information in the memoranda indicated that Japan would probably not be able to continue the struggle beyond the autumn.

As the Japanese correctly guessed American intentions, so U.S. Intelligence officers deduced Japanese strategy, and

△ *A scene that would be all too frequent during the attack on Japan:* kamikaze *attack.*

could be given of any impending *kamikaze* attack, so that perhaps the aircraft could be destroyed on the ground. Close fighter cover would be provided for convoys to ward off *kamikazes*. Submarines were to give notice of attacks from Korean bases. By these means then, and by the anti-aircraft fire from the ships themselves, it was hoped to reduce the damage done by *kamikazes*. In any case, as they were a wasting asset, the intensity of the attacks was expected to drop as the operation continued. And although the short distances the *kamikazes* would have to fly would make them difficult to intercept, the disruption of communications and the failure of the Japanese to establish a combined air headquarters would be factors working against their success. Also, at this point, the *kamikaze* pilots were no longer all volunteers, the available planes were not as suitable as earlier *kamikaze* craft, and fuel was in short supply.

As for the water-borne suicide craft, these had not proved highly effective at Okinawa, and with regard to the invasion of Japan, the "Olympic" plan included heavy attacks on their potential bases.

In conclusion, the raising of the divisions to meet the invasion exhausted all Japan's manpower reserves. Many soldiers expected to fight and resist the invaders were poorly trained and badly equipped. In fact the Japanese encountered such difficulty in providing the Kyūshū defenders with adequate weapons that their ability to resist a landing was imperilled. There was also a serious shortage of experienced officers, and most of the technical units were without experienced tradesmen. There were only enough reserve supplies for a limited period, and both fighting formations and lines of communication were short of transport; much of what was available was animal-drawn. Fuel was in extremely short supply.

In comparison, the U.S. 6th Army comprised fully-equipped and experienced veteran formations. The Allied air forces had air supremacy over Japan and would have had no difficulty in disrupting Japanese communications, and any attempts to move reserves.

However, the Americans realised that the invasion of Kyūshū would quite likely result in such a resurgence of national spirit, that the Japanese would be fanatical in their fight to the death to defend every inch of ground, as they had done at Okinawa.

▽ *Cabbage cultivation in the centre of Tokyo, on sites of bomb-destroyed buildings.*

American plans henceforth contained elaborate provisions to counter *kamikaze* air attacks which could theoretically wipe out the invasion convoys. At Okinawa, overhead fighters had shot down some 60 per cent of attacking *kamikazes*, and anti-aircraft fire accounted for a further 20 per cent. The remaining *kamikazes*, however, had wrought considerable havoc. It was therefore planned that, commencing eight days before the preliminary phase of Operation "Olympic", American aircraft were to locate and attack concealed *kamikaze* bases. Bombing of all known *kamikaze* airstrips within 300 miles of the assault area was to take place in the hope of reducing the *kamikaze* threat by about one-fifth. B-24 and B-32 aircraft were to patrol selected areas containing known Japanese bases, so that early warning

The words "Secret Weapons" have an emotive ring which disguises the fact that they are generally unusual weapons developed secretly whose employment comes as a nasty surprise to the enemy.

German research in World War II was affected by the early victories in the opening years: it seemed that the Reich would be able to win the war with her conventional weapons, and so there was little call for research in new equipment. Thus many of the projects which were developed

GERMANY'S SECRET WEAPONS

were done on a freelance basis by German companies.

It is an awesome thought that in 1939 the Germans had already established a research group into the possibilities of atomic power and, moreover, that they had a three-year advantage over the Allies. Rivalry between the physicists and a failure to "sell" their work to *Reichsminister* Speer meant that they never received the massive backing which was accorded the "Manhattan Project". Up to 1942 both sides had reached the same point in their work, but from there on the Germans marked time.

In rocketry, however, they made major advances. In 1945, when V-2's were falling on Britain, a British Government statement admitted that "the design and the construction of the V2 is undoubtedly a considerable achievement", but added "the military value of the weapon at present is extremely doubtful". Had a V-2 been armed with an atomic warhead, the missile would certainly have caused the panic that Hitler had envisaged.

Research had begun before the war, but unlike the work of the nuclear physicists it was centralised and under firm leadership. Walter Dornberger, an experienced artillery officer and a professional engineer who became head of the rocket research project, laid down the missile's specifications. It was to have a payload of about a ton and a range of at least 160 miles, so representing an advance on the largest guns of World War I.

German work was interrupted by heavy air raids on the research centre at Peenemünde, and earlier in 1943 when Hitler ordered a cutback in supplies after suffering from a bad dream on the subject of rockets.

There were two major projects, the A4 (V-2) ballistic missile and the FZG 76 (V-1) flying bomb. The V-2 has always attracted more interest than the V-1 as it was a proper rocket, whereas the V-1 was a pulse-jet-powered pilotless aeroplane with a 1,870-pound warhead. However, in value for

◄ *The Bachem Ba 349A "Natter" (Adder) on its launching rails (left) and just after launching (right). This was designed late in 1944 as a last-ditch interceptor fighter. Powered by four rocket engines, the* Natter *had a top speed of 560 mph and a climb rate of 35,800 feet per minute. Armament was twenty-four 55-mm rockets under a detachable nose cone. None was used operationally.*
▼ *The high command inspects progress at Peenemünde in 1944. From left to right: General W. Warlimont (Keitel's deputy), Field-Marshal W. Keitel, General F. Fromm, and Major-General Dr. W. Dornberger, head of the Peenemünde establishment.*

◄ *The early days at Peenemünde: a* Waffenamt *(Army Weapons Department) inspection in 1942. Among those present are Dornberger (back to camera), Dr. W. Herrmann, in charge of the supersonic wind tunnel (background, in civilian clothes), Lieutenant-General Schneider, head of the* Waffenamt *(with binoculars), and Dr. Wernher von Braun, the rocket engine designer (foreground, in civilian clothes). Overleaf: Potentially Germany's most important weapon – the V-2 (or A4) guided missile. The one seen here is a captured example, lifting off from the White Sands proving ground, New Mexico, on May 10, 1946.*

◄◄ *Five views of a German V-weapon factory. The need for secrecy, and the steady growth of Allied bombing capabilities, meant that more and more production centres had to be hidden away underground towards the end of the war. Seen here is a V-2 factory in a village north-west of Berlin. Above the ground (top) it had the appearance of just another little village. But underground (four bottom views) the factory consisted of large galleries in which V-2 components were assembled by slave labourers. Even had such factories been detected, there was little the Allies could have done.*

◄ *German groundcrew make last-minute adjustments to a V-2 in preparation for an operational firing against southern England.*

▽ *The motor of the 10th experimental A4 blows up after 2½ seconds of running, as a result of a servicing error, on January 7, 1943 at Test Stand No. 7.*

▽▽ *Moments later the wrecked missile topples over onto its side. The quartered black and white markings were to aid the photo-telemetry equipment.*

2985

2986

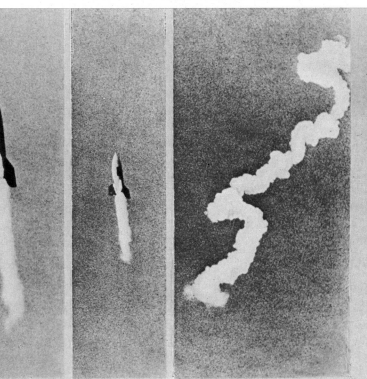

◁ *A V-2 lifts off and accelerates swiftly into its ballistic trajectory. Control of the missile was dependent on a stable platform in the nose. This contained two gyroscopes, one defining the pitch axis and the other the yaw and roll axes. Any deviation from the planned trajectory was detected by these gyroscopes, and corrections to reduce the error to zero fed to the control vanes on the fins and in the rocket efflux.*
▽ *V-2 launch site.*

money the V-1 more than repaid the German efforts. Germany expended an estimated £12,600,670 on the manufacture and launching of V-1's and the erection and defence of the sites. The flying-bomb offensive between June 12 and September 1, 1944 cost the British £47,635,190 in lost production, loss of aircraft and crews, in extra A.A. defences, in clearance of damage, and in the bombing attacks on the launching sites. In addition, permanent repairs to housing damaged by the V-1's cost at least another £25,000,000. The V-1 had a very high blast effect when filled with *Trialen*, an explosive with almost twice the power of the conventional RDX-type.

A V-2 cost £12,000 compared with a V-1's £125. The most serious damage done by the V-2 was in fact inflicted on the Germans: "The A4 project critically invaded Germany's aircraft production capacity; the induced shortage of electrical components from the summer of 1943 onwards not only crippled the fighter-aircraft industry, but interfered severely with both submarine and radar requirements." Moreover, Speer refused to allow work to expand on the anti-aircraft rocket projects late in 1944 unless the V-2 programme was cut back to provide the necessary components.

Had the resources used on the V-2 been diverted to an anti-aircraft missile, Allied bombers would have sustained very heavy losses. In December 1944 a committee under Dornberger reviewed the work on anti-aircraft missiles. They awarded three contracts, for the "*Wasserfall*", "*Schmetterling*" and Ruhrstahl X-4.

This last missile was to have been used by German fighters against B-17 formations. It was a wire-guided liquid-fuelled rocket with a 44-lb warhead. One of its major features was the use of non-strategic materials and components which could be constructed and assembled by unskilled labour. The metal sheets had simple tabs which, like a metal toy, could be slotted together. The wings were of plywood and were secured to aluminium supports by nuts and bolts.

By February 1945, some 1,300 missiles were on the production lines when the engines at the BMW factory at Stargard were destroyed in an air raid. The work that was necessary to re-build the plant was so great that the project was allowed to lapse.

2988

◁◁ *British troops examine a* Reichenberg *suicide aircraft captured at Tramm, near Danneberg. This was a piloted V-1 "doodlebug". None was flown operationally, although 175 were built.*

△ *V-1 launching site overrun by the Canadians in Holland. Inspecting the ramp are Lance-Corporal Don Stover of Moose Jaw, Saskatchewan, and Sergeant R. Clarke of Forestdale, B.C.*

◁ *Launching ramp taken by the British in France.*

▽ *Underground V-1 (FZG-76) factory at Nordhausen, captured by the 1st Army in April 1945.*

▷ and ▽ *The Holzbrau-Kissing* Enzian *ground-to-air missile. This was based on the Me 163 fighter, and 38 test models were fired before the project was cancelled in January 1945.*
▷▷ *The* Do *missile. This extraordinary missile was designed to be launched from a submerged U-boat. But after unofficial trials from U-511 in 1942, the project was abandoned.*
△▷ *and* ▷▽ *The Rheinmetall* Rheinbote *surface-to-surface missile. This had an adequate range of 140 miles, but a completely useless payload of 44 pounds of high explosive. None was fired operationally.*

The "*Wasserfall*" missile was designed by the Peenemünde team which had worked on the V-2. It was liquid-fuelled and could reach a maximum altitude of 55,000 feet.

The "*Schmetterling*" anti-aircraft missile incorporated features of the Hs 293 glider bomb. It had two solid-fuel booster rockets and a liquid-fuel engine which could take it to a maximum altitude of 45,000 feet. With a 51-lb warhead it was intended to be the standard anti-aircraft missile for the Reich.

As the war swung against Germany there was an increased emphasis on the use of non-strategic materials. The Me 262 had demonstrated the effectiveness of jet-propelled fighters to the *Reichsluftfahrtministerium* (Air Ministry). In September 1944 the R.L.M. called for a high-performance fighter utilising a minimum of strategic materials and suitable for mass production by semi-skilled labour, and which could be ready for production by January 1945.

The Heinkel He 162A "Salamander", popularly known as the "*Volksjäger*" or People's Fighter, was submitted to the Ministry. A scale mock-up was inspected on September 23, 1944, and five days later a quantity order was awarded. The prototype flew for the first time on December 6, 1944. In a demonstration four days later it crashed in front of Party functionaries and members of the Ministry, but despite this development continued.

Its components reflect the raw materials' famine that existed in Germany at the end of the war. The one-piece wing was of wooden construction and the fuselage had duralumin formers and skin with a plywood nose and a tail of duralumin, steel, and wood.

Not only was there a lack of raw materials, but the Reich had a shrinking labour force as men were drafted into the Army. Unlike Britain, Germany never fully mobilised its considerable pool of female labour. Instead she employed foreign workers, the bulk of whom had been shipped against their will from occupied countries. Predictably, the quality of the workmanship was low.

At the far end of the scale from the V-2, a rocket which served to further political rather than tactical ends, there was a wide variety of field rocket equipment.

Chemical warfare units equipped with the 10-cm *Nebelwerfer*

35 had participated in the invasion of Poland. At the beginning of the war there were few *Nebeltruppen*, but the low cost of rocket artillery made it attractive to the Germans. Moreover, rocket batteries had an impressive rate of fire: a brigade could fire 108 rounds in ten seconds or 648 rounds in 90 seconds.

The Germans developed a variety of rocket projectiles, from the 181-pound 28-cm *Wurfkörper Spreng* which could be fired from its crate or a mobile launcher, to the anti-tank *Panzerfaust*. This weapon was a small hollow-charge rocket fired from a tube.

The hollow charge principle had attracted Hitler before the war and he had suggested that it could be employed against the bunkers and emplacements in Eben Emaël, the fort which was in 1940 the key to the Belgian defences.

Hitler's interference in German research led to considerable funds being diverted to prestige projects. At a demonstration of the 80-cm railway gun "*Gustav*", Guderian was horrified to hear Dr. Müller of Krupps tell Hitler that the massive gun could be used against tanks. "For a moment I was dumbfounded as I

envisaged the mass-production of 'Gustavs'." He hurriedly explained to Hitler that the gun could be fired, but could certainly never hit a tank and moreover needed 45 minutes to reload between shots.

"Gustav" was a good example of the German interest in superheavy versions of conventional weapons. The gun, which required a crew of 1,420 for its operation and defence, was commanded by a major-general. It has two types of shell: a four-ton anti-personnel projectile with a range of 29 miles, and a 17-ton concrete-piercing shell with a range of 23 miles. The gun was employed at Sevastopol' and Warsaw and fired a total of about 60 or 70 shots.

As a piece of ordnance engineering it was undeniably a considerable achievement, but it was also a waste of resources, for a bomber could have achieved the same results at less cost.

One artillery project which might have paid for the effort which was expended on it was the "V-3" "High-Pressure Pump". Sited at Mimoyecques on the French coast, the gun was designed to fire a finned 300-pound shell at London. It was unusual in that the powder for the charge was distributed in a series of breeches

△ ◁ ◁ *Superheavy German ordnance. With a good railway system at her disposal, Germany found the development of such monsters worthwhile.*
△ ◁ *Three views of a German rocket gun in action.*
◁ *Rocket artillery, in which the Germans led the world all through the war.*
△ ▷ *An American soldier poses beside an experimental rocket launcher abandoned by the Germans. It was a very neat piece of design, and had a plastic shield to protect the firer from the blast.*
▷ *The incredible Hochdruckpumpe long-range gun. This was built into the ground at a fixed elevation and bearing, and used arrow-shaped projectiles, 8 feet long and 150 lbs in weight. The barrel was in 40 sections, and there were 28 powder chambers distributed along the bore. The intention was that as the projectile moved up the barrel, the extra powder chambers would fire in succession, to boost the shell to a muzzle velocity of 4,500 feet per second. Range was about 80 miles. The barrel burst about every third shot, however.*

1.

2.

3.

4.

5.

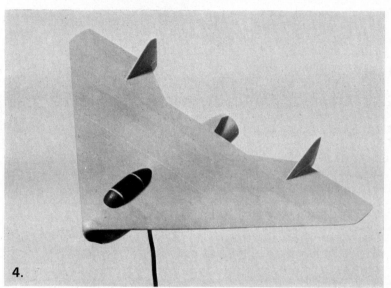

6.

1. *The Focke-Wulf Ta 183 fighter (4 × 30-mm cannon; 597 mph), about to enter production as the war ended.* **2.** *The Blohm & Voss P.215 bad weather fighter* (7 × 30- and 1 × 20-mm cannon and 2 × 1,100-lb bombs; 594 mph). **3.** *Blohm & Voss P.192 ground-attack aircraft (2 × 30- and 2 × 20-mm cannon and 1 ×* 1,100-lb bomb) with the propeller behind the cockpit. **4.** *The Arado E.581.4 fighter (2 × 30-mm cannon).* **5.** *The Focke-Wulf Ta 183 (Project II) fighter, with a* more conventional empennage. **6.** *The Junkers 287 bomber (8,800 lbs of bombs; 550 mph).*

7.

8.

9.

10.

11.

12.

7. *The Arado bad weather fighter Project I (6 × 30-mm cannon and 2 × 1,100-lb bombs; 503 mph).* 8. *The Blohm & Voss P.207.03 pusher fighter (3 × 30-mm* cannon; 490 mph).* 9. *The Focke-Wulf Ta 283 athodyd fighter (2 × 30-mm cannon; 682 mph).* 10. *The Arado E.340 bomber (3,300 lbs of bombs; 388* mph).* 11. *The Blohm & Voss P.194 attack aircraft (2 × 30- and 2 × 20-mm cannon and 1 × 2,200-lb bomb; 482 mph).* 12. *The Arado miniature fighter, carried* by the Ar 234C bomber (1 × 30-mm cannon). Span was 16 feet 5 inches.*

△ *The remarkable Heinkel He 111Z* Zwilling *glider tug. This was an amalgamation of two He 111H-6 bombers, joined by a new centre section carrying a fifth engine, to tow the mammoth Me 321 Gigant transport glider. The crew was in the port fuselage of the* Zwilling. *The basic H-6 variant was also used for the launching of various air-launched missiles such as the* Fritz X *and* Hagelhorn. *It was also used for trials with the* Friedensengel *experimental winged torpedo.*

along the barrel. As the shell moved up the barrel each charge would be fired to increase the shell's speed. This was not only economical in propellant, but the barrels suffered less wear.

The original scheme had called for 25 barrels located on the French coast, firing one round every 12 seconds.

Work was well advanced on the site at Mimoyecques: 100 feet down in the limestone hill there was a warren of tunnels and galleries served by a railway line.

In tests, however, the barrel had a tendency to burst after several rounds had been fired. The shells, too, proved to be unstable when they reached velocities above 3,300

feet per second. *Reichsminister* Speer was confident that with better materials and workmanship, and more wind tunnel experiments on the shell, the gun could be made a viable weapon. This confidence, however, was not shared by some of the army artillery experts.

German inventiveness was extremely fertile before and during the war. Some of the projects were pursued to a successful, if expensive conclusion, while others were either left on the drawing board or remained to be captured as mock-ups or prototypes. Among these ideas were the artificial creation of an aerial vortex to destroy Allied bombers. An amplifier which would project sound waves of high power and low frequency was built and tested. (The noise was intended to kill or disorientate a man.) A piloted version of the V-1 was constructed and a squadron of dedicated pilots was formed. They were not employed because no target worth their sacrifice appeared before the end of the war. The "Do" missile, a submarine-launched solid-fuelled rocket, was successfully fired from a submerged U-boat. There were plans for U-boats to tow V-2's to positions off the United States coast and fire them from special canis-

ters. A more modest weapon was developed for close quarter fighting in tanks. The *Sturmgewehr* 44, in itself an important advance in small arms technology, was fitted with a periscope. With this special sight the gun incorporated a curved barrel. Tests, however, showed that the bullets were distorted by the barrel.

Hitler's interference in German research misdirected several projects, but his interest in the jet-propelled Me 262 was disastrous.

The aircraft was designed to be a high-speed interceptor. With two Junkers Jumo 004B-1, 2, or 3 turbojets it had a maximum speed of 538 mph, which put it out of range of the fastest conventional fighters the Allies possessed. Its four 30-mm cannon and 24 R4M air-to-air missiles gave it a fire-power which could have restored control of the skies over Germany to the Luftwaffe.

Hitler, however, saw this fighter as a new revenge weapon. "This will be my Blitz bomber," he said when he was told that it could carry bombs. From the "*Schwalbe*" it became the "*Sturmvogel*", from speeding "Swallow" to lumbering "Storm Bird" loaded with two 550-pound bombs. This load not only made the aircraft difficult to handle, but put back the project

by at least four months. When the *Sturmvogel* was employed in action it was slow enough to be pursued and attacked by piston-engined fighters.

The Luftwaffe eventually received a real jet bomber in the Arado Ar 234 "*Blitz*". It arrived too late to affect the fighting in Europe, though one was reported to have flown a photo-reconnaissance mission along Britain's east coast.

Germany's research and development programme was diffuse and ill co-ordinated, suffering from interference by Hitler and no proper central scientific control. Many projects received backing only because their originators were able to "sell" them to some government ministry. Party functionaries in some unusual ministries fancied themselves as the patrons of scientific research and granted money and resources to German inventors.

However, some of the fruits of German war-time research remain with us today. The V-2's which were shipped to the United States in 1945 were the beginning of the American space programme. The "short" 7.62-mm round for the MP43 and 44 assault rifles, became the basis for the current Russian AK47 assault rifle.

CHAPTER 177
Russia's war against Japan
by William Fowler

At midnight on August 8, 1945, the Japanese Ambassador in Moscow, Naotake Sato, received the Soviet declaration of war. Ten minutes later, on the other side of the Soviet Union, 1,500,000 Russian troops were launched on the last great offensive of the war.

Together with 5,500 armoured vehicles and nearly 4,000 aircraft, these forces would give a spectacular demonstration of mobile war against the 1,040,000 men of the Kwantung Army in Manchuria.

Throughout the war neither the Russians nor the Japanese had made any offensive moves—indeed Japan had taken great care to honour the Neutrality Pact of April 1941. On the strength of reports from their spy in Toyko, Richard Sorge, the Russian high command began to

▽ *Soviet T-34's and other vehicles roar over the Russo-Japanese border at the beginning of the war in the Far East. A liaison aircraft banks over the column.*

transfer men from the Far East as the war with Germany grew more intense.

In June 1941 the Russians had about 30 reasonably well equipped divisions in the Far East. Japanese Intelligence estimated that during the crucial period between June and December 1941, the Russians transferred 15 infantry divisions, three cavalry divisions, 1,700 tanks, and 1,500 aircraft to the German front.

New units were mobilised to replace them, including nine infantry divisions and four brigades and an air army headquarters. By December 1941 the Japanese estimate, which was fairly accurate, was that Russian strength stood at about 800,000 men, 1,000 tanks, and 1,000 aircraft. In fact by the end of 1942, when the last major transfers ceased, the Soviet order of battle stood at 19 infantry divisions, ten infantry brigades, 750,000 men, 1,000 tanks, and 1,000 aircraft – although of course these units were neither at a state of full readiness, nor completely trained.

These unit strengths remained about the same until the end of 1944. Training conditions were as harsh as the climate, and the armies had a low priority for re-equipment. In 1942, however, the garrisons in northern Sakhalin and Kamchatka were increased after the Japanese had captured Attu and Kiska.

Just as the numbers and quality of the Russian troops stationed in the Far East reflected the fortunes of war in Europe, so too as the war swung against Japan, the Kwantung Army began to serve as a pool for reinforcements.

Japanese strength in Manchuria reached its peak in January 1942, when the army stood at 1.1 million men. During 1942 and 1943 they were still able to equal at least 70 per cent of Soviet strength in the Far East. During 1944 many troops, including almost all the élite units, were gradually withdrawn to Japan. By July they were at their weakest, with only seven divisions in Manchuria.

These forces were increased and by August 9, 1945 there were 24 divisions and 11 brigades in Manchuria, seven divisions in Korea, and one brigade on Sakhalin and in the Kuriles. Total strength, including Manchukuan and Inner Mongolian satellite forces, stood at just over one million men, of which 787,600 were in the Kwantung Army. The Japanese had 1,215 armoured vehicles, 1,800 aircraft, and 6,700 guns and mortars. However, this equipment was almost all obsolete, and the Kwantung Army was a shadow of the well trained veteran force which had existed early in 1942. All the first line equipment and trained troops had been posted to the Pacific, and the most seasoned unit had only been established in the spring of 1944.

The Kwantung Army was brought up to numerical strength about ten days before the Soviet attack, when in a hurried mobilisation eight of its 24 divisions and seven of the nine infantry brigades, that is over one-quarter of the total Japanese military manpower in Manchuria, were formed from all the remaining Japanese males in the area. Until then they had been exempt from military duty, being unfit or over-age. One of the two weak

tank brigades was formed in July 1945.

Although the standard Japanese infantry division had about 23,000 men, the actual strengths of those in Manchuria ranged between 11,000 and 15,000. Even divisions transferred from China were not complete: many had only one of the nine artillery companies prescribed per division.

Weapons too were inadequate: there was no artillery heavier than 75-mm, no modern anti-tank guns, and the tanks were very light, thinly-armoured, and under-armed.

The 2nd Air Army had a front line strength of only 225 fighters, 40 bombers, 45 reconnaissance, and 20 *kamikaze* aircraft, with 640 training aircraft in reserve. Most of these aircraft, moreover, were obsolete.

There was a shortage of ammunition, and the number of medium and light machine guns with infantry units was less than half the authorised figure. The Japanese estimated that the average efficiency of each division was not greater than three-tenths of that of a pre-war first line division. The morale of both officers and men was low, particularly in the newly formed units.

Russia prepares

By 1943 the Western Allies had contained the Germans and Japanese and forced them on to the defensive. The Soviet Union and the United States began to discuss the possibility of Soviet entry into the war in the Far East. Stalin agreed in principle, and plans were made to enlarge the denuded armies in the east.

Between the Teheran Conference and the end of the war in Europe in May 1945, the Soviet High Command, or *Stavka*, reorganised the two "fronts" in the area, the Transbaikal and the Far East.

They were re-equipped with new tanks and guns, and stocks of ammunition, fuel, and supplies were moved up in great secrecy.

From April to August the Russians moved 30 divisions, nine brigades, and other units from Europe. The Japanese estimated that the Russians had moved only 20 to 45 divisions and that the total strength of Soviet forces by the end of July 1945 was between 40 and 45 divisions. Japanese Intelligence expected the Russians to build up a force of 60 divisions

▽ The Transbaikal Front: motorised and cavalry units of the 53rd Army approach the foot-hills of the Hsingan range.
▽ ◁ A pontoon bridge erected by engineers of the 5th Army over the River Mudantsuan.
▽ ▽ Animal- and man-power are mobilised to assist a cart across a wide and muddy arm of a river in northern Manchuria.

before attacking, and so they concluded that the Russians would not be ready until early August.

Soviet forces were divided between three Fronts, comprising 11 combined-arms armies, one tank army, and three air armies, in all 80 divisions, four tank and mechanised corps, 40 independent tank and mechanised brigades, and six infantry brigades. The total strength of the army and air force was 1,577,725 men (of whom 1,058,982 were front line troops), 26,137 guns and mortars, 3,704 tanks, and 1,852 self-propelled guns (the Japanese estimated 4,500 tanks), with 5,368 aircraft−including naval−of which 4,807 were combat aircraft (the Japanese estimated 6,300).

The Russian superiority was qualitative as well as quantitative. They had sent four of their most experienced armies from the European theatre. The 5th and the 39th had been in action at Königsberg in East Prussia and had a reputation for dealing with fixed defences and fortifications. The other two armies, the 6th Guards Tank Army and the 53rd Army, came from the 2nd Ukrainian Front, and were capable "Blitzkrieg" campaigners.

With these veterans came experienced commanders. Head of the new *Stavka* for Soviet Forces in the Far East was Marshal Aleksandr M. Vasilevsky, recently Chief of the General Staff. Colonel-General S. P. Ivanov became chief-of-staff for the new command. Of the three fronts, Marshal Rodion Ya. Malinovsky commanded the Transbaikal Front, Marshal Kyril A. Meretskov the 1st Far Eastern Front and General of the Army Maxim A. Purkaev the 2nd Far Eastern Front. Purkaev had

been the Far Eastern commander through much of the Russo-German war. The Pacific Fleet came under Admiral Ivan S. Yumashev.

This new leadership was necessary because most of the officers in the old Far East Army had only seen action in 1941 in disorganised rear-guard actions against the Germans. They were also inexperienced in the tactics of massed armoured penetration with air support.

Swift and ruthless as the Soviet attack might be, the preparations for the operation in Manchuria are no less impressive.

For three and a half months the trans-Siberian railway was used to its maximum capacity, as men from Europe made the long journey to their new assembly areas (anything from 4,000 to 7,000 miles). Nearly 750,000 men made the journey, and between May and July 136,000 truck loads of equipment were sent east. To save the railway, all motorised units of the Transbaikal Front moved independently from the Chita-Karymskaya sector to the concentration areas in eastern Mongolia, a distance of 625 to 750 miles, mostly over desert. Even the infantry of the 17th and 36th Armies marched the last 150 to 300 miles.

The 6th Guards Tank Army left its tanks and assault guns in Czechoslovakia for other units, and at Choibalsan in Mongolia collected over 600 new vehicles sent directly from the Ural armaments fact-

◁ ◁ ◁ *Soviet infantry watch from their start line as an artillery barrage softens up a defended village on the second day of the offensive.*
◁ ◁ *T-34's, secure from air attack, advance in a cloud of dust and exhaust fumes. The Russians had not only a superiority in numbers, but also a qualitative advantage over the Japanese tanks.*
◁ *Infantry assault a Japanese position. Despite their lack of equipment, the Japanese put up a spirited defence at many points.*

ories. An ingenious idea in principle, it caused some disruption because of the short time allocated to the tank crews to collect their vehicles from the depot.

As with most Soviet operations, ammunition had priority in the build-up of reserves. Tank munitions topped the list, with artillery and mortar ammunition second and infantry ammunition third. Food for 15 days was stocked, but the petrol, oil, and lubricants amassed proved to be inadequate when the operation got under way.

Water was a special problem, because troops of the Transbaikal Front would have to cross the Gobi Desert before they reached the Great Hsingan mountain range. Engineer battalions and other units dug some 635 wells in the concentration and staging areas. Vehicles were loaded with water, fuel, and spares for the journey across the desert. In view of the known prevalence of epidemic diseases in northern China, all Soviet troops were inoculated against plague and other ailments.

As its occupation of eastern Europe had demonstrated, the Soviet Union did not fight simply to defeat the enemy and end the war. At the Yalta Conference in February 1945, President Roosevelt and Marshal Stalin came to a private agreement. Stalin would declare war on Japan three months after the end of the war in Europe, subject to the successful conclusion of a treaty with China; Soviet troops would operate in Chinese territory, Japanese-occupied Manchuria, and Jehol. In return for this, Stalin demanded American recognition of Soviet territorial claims in the Pacific: Russia was to have

the Kurile Islands, the southern part of Sakhalin Island, and the old Russian bases of Port Arthur and Dairen in south Manchuria. Stalin even persuaded Roosevelt to approach the Nationalist Chinese Government on his behalf to secure Chiang Kai-shek's acceptance of these conditions.

When on July 21 President Truman remarked to Stalin at the Potsdam Conference that the Allies had a new weapon of special destructive force, the Soviet leader showed no real interest but said he hoped the Allies would make "good use of it against the Japanese".

Whether Stalin realised the impact that the first atomic bomb would have on the Japanese is difficult to say. Vasilevsky confirmed, after the war, that September had been fixed for the start of the offensive. The general staff was troubled when it was told in May that August 8 would be D-day. Finally, in a telephone call from Potsdam, Stalin told Vasilevsky to push the date forward to August 1. The Marshal explained that the state of preparation did not permit this, and so the two leaders finally agreed on August 9.

The troops may have been in position by August 9, but Japanese Intelligence had not been completely wrong when it predicted a later date for the offensive. Soviet logistic support was severely strained by the operation, and many tanks were halted by lack of fuel, which had to be flown in in an extemporised re-supply operation.

It was probably Stalin's military and political intuition which made him realise that the war would soon be over, with or without an atomic bomb, and that if he wanted land in the east he would have to act fast. With this land he took nearly 600,000 Japanese prisoners-of-war, who were sent to the Soviet Union and Mongolia as forced labour. Between 1948 and 1950, 513,139 were repatriated.

Despite the steady reduction of Japan's empire by land and air, culminating in the destruction of Hiroshima and Nagasaki, Soviet historians claim that Japan surrendered because of Russia's entry into the war. Ignoring this assertion, let us examine the Red Army's contribution to the war in the Far East.

Two-fold offensive

The plans were fairly simple, but some parts of the execution were complicated and bold. The two main thrusts would be made by the Transbaikal Front from the west, cutting through most of Manchuria to Ch'ang-ch'un and Mukden, and by the 1st Far Eastern Front from the east, breaking through the fortifications facing the Maritime Province and moving to Kirin and on to Ch'ang-ch'un. The 2nd Far Eastern Front in the north would breach the Amur and make a thrust up the Sungari towards Harbin.

The main weight of the Soviet forces was Malinovsky's Transbaikal Front, which was deployed mainly in Mongolia. Between May and July the Marshal, his staff, and the entire 6th Guards Tank and 53rd Armies had been transferred from Prague to the grim landscape of Siberia and Mongolia.

At the same time the 39th Army had been transferred from Insterburg. They joined the 36th and 17th Armies already garrisoned in Siberia.

The Transbaikal Front comprised these five armies, with the supporting 12th Air Army (1,334 aircraft) under Marshal of Aviation S. A. Khudyakov, and a joint Russian and Mongolian composite "Cavalry-Mechanised Group", which was about six divisions of mostly horsed cavalry. Nearly half the Soviet strength in the Far East was assigned to this front, which was defended by light Japanese forces.

The Russian plans were based on the assumption, which subsequently proved to be correct, that the Japanese would not expect an attack to come across hundreds of miles of the Gobi Desert in Inner Mongolia and over the Great Hsingan mountain range. Indeed the Japanese forces were concentrated for a counter-attack in the Manchurian plain, and only small garrisons had been placed in the towns around Hailar, near the Soviet border. It was not only the Japanese who thought that the plan was unlikely; long-serving officers from the Red Army in the East regarded a crossing of the Gobi in August as near suicidal. For their pessimism they were relegated to the posts of deputy commanders.

In the Maritime Province, the 1st Far Eastern Front faced an equally daunting barrier, for here the Japanese expected an offensive. They had begun building permanent fortifications over 20 years earlier. The defences were from eight to 15 miles deep and set in difficult country among mountains, extinct volcanoes, steep river valleys, and patches of thick woodland. In the centre the 35th Army would have to cross the marshy valley of the Ussuri river, while to the south the 25th Army would tackle the formidable fortifications on the Manchurian border with Korea, notably the fortress area of Dunnin.

Meretskov decided to allocate most of his supporting artillery and armour to the 5th Army, under Colonel-General N. I. Krylov. Supported by the 1st Army on its right, its 12 divisions would plough into the Japanese defensive system around Mutan-chiang, north-west of Vladivostok.

In conjunction with these land operations, the Pacific Fleet was instructed to disrupt Japanese maritime communications, prevent the use of the northern Korean ports, and assist the army in preventing any Japanese landings in the Soviet Union. Later it received the additional mission, which proved to be its most important, of mounting amphibious assaults on the Japanese ports in northern Korea, southern Sakhalin, and the northern Kurile Islands.

The fleet consisted of two "Kirov"-class cruisers, a destroyer leader with 10 destroyers, 19 destroyer escorts, 49 submarine chasers, 78 submarines, and 204 M.T.B.s. In addition there were 1,549 land-based aircraft of Fleet Aviation under Lieutenant-General Piotr N. Lemeshko.

Japanese forces consisted of one old light cruiser, one destroyer, 45 small patrol minesweepers, and 170 aircraft, most of which were to remain in the northern bases of the Japanese home islands.

△ The citizens of Harbin greet the men of the 1st Far Eastern Front. The Japanese surrender spared the city the horrors of street fighting, and saved the Russians from a protracted campaign in the east. After the surrender, the Manchurian campaign became a logistical operation to move men quickly into those areas which had ceased to be under Japanese control. Aircraft were used to transport ad hoc airborne units to capture towns in advance of the land forces.

The Transbaikal Front

But let us return to the Transbaikal
Front where Soviet forces were building
up stocks of ammunition, and sweltering
in the August sun.

The 500 miles from Tamsag Bulag to
the Kwantung Army headquarters at
Ch'ang-ch'un, and on to Mukden, would
be travelled without a break. The first
task of the 6th Guards Tank Army was to
cross the Great Hsingan range and reach
the line Lu-pei–Li-chuan in five days.
Emphasis was placed on the need to cross
the mountains before the Japanese had
time to react and deploy their reserves,
which were known to be some 200 to 250
miles from their western frontier.

The 6th Guards Tank Army, under
Colonel-General A. G. Kravchenko, would
have the 39th Army, under Lieutenant-
General I. I. Lyudnikov, on its left flank,
facing the fortifications at A-erh-shan; on
the right the 17th Army, under Lieutenant-
General A. I. Danilov, would face the
desert and mountains around Linh-sia
and Chihfeng. The 53rd Army, under
Colonel-General I. M. Managarov, would
be held in reserve. In the north the 36th
Army, under Lieutenant-General A. A.
Luchinsky, would make supporting
attacks on Hailar and towards Tsitsihar,
while in the south the Soviet-Mongolian
Cavalry-Mechanised Group, under

Colonel-General I. A. Pliev, would thrust towards Ch'eng-te and Kalgan (Chiang-chia-k'ou).

Some units like the 36th and 17th Armies were accustomed to the Far East, while the joint Cavalry-Mechanised Group had been locally raised. Other armies had a local Siberian motorised infantry division attached, except for the 6th Guards Tank Army, which had two.

Since it would bear the full weight of the operation, the 6th Guards Tank Army was given more than the usual mechanised infantry complement. It had two reinforced mechanised infantry corps, one tank corps, two motorised infantry divisions, two assault gun brigades, and four independent tank brigades. Its total strength stood at 826 tanks and 193 assault guns; this included 615 late model T-34 tanks (the remainder were older T-26, BT-5, and BT-7 tanks), 188 armoured cars, 6,489 other vehicles, and 948 motorcycles. It was supported by 995 field guns and heavy mortars, 43 *Katyusha* rocket-launchers, and 165 anti-aircraft guns. In all, it comprised some 44 motorised rifle and 25 tank battalions.

Drawing on the experience of their own and German mechanised operations in Europe, the Russians arranged for motorcycle and air reconnaissance to cover the flanks and point of their armies. Aircraft covered the area from 30 to 60 miles ahead, while motorcycles operated between 45 to 50 miles in advance. Each of these reinforced motorcycle battalions carried powerful radio transmitters.

Flank reconnaissance covered points 15 miles out, an important provision since there would be gaps between the armies, and even within the 6th Guards Tank Army the two columns would be separated by nearly 50 miles.

Opposite this carefully-balanced force stood the Japanese 3rd Area Army under General K. Ushiroku, consisting of the 30th and 44th Armies. Their task was to defend the Ch'ang-ch'un–Ssu-p'ing-chieh –Seoul, and the Mukden–Dairen railways with the industrial centres located along them. They had permission to retreat to the fortified lines in the T'ung-hua area.

The 44th Army, under Lieutenant-General Y. Hongo, with headquarters at Liaoyuan, had positioned its three divisions and one tank brigade to cover the Inner and Outer Mongolian borders from A-erh-shan in the north through Taonan to Tungliao in the south. The 30th Army, under Lieutenant-General S. Iida (who had commanded the Japanese army which invaded Burma in 1942) had its headquarters at Mei-hok'ou, with four divisions covering Ch'ang-ch'un and the fortified zone.

Ushiroku retained one division, three independent mixed brigades, and a tank brigade in reserve near Mukden, and another at Jehol in south-west Manchuria.

The 4th Army, under Lieutenant-General M. Uemura, with headquarters at Tsitsihar, was composed of three divisions and four independent mixed brigades. Their task was to cover northern Manchuria. One division and an inde-

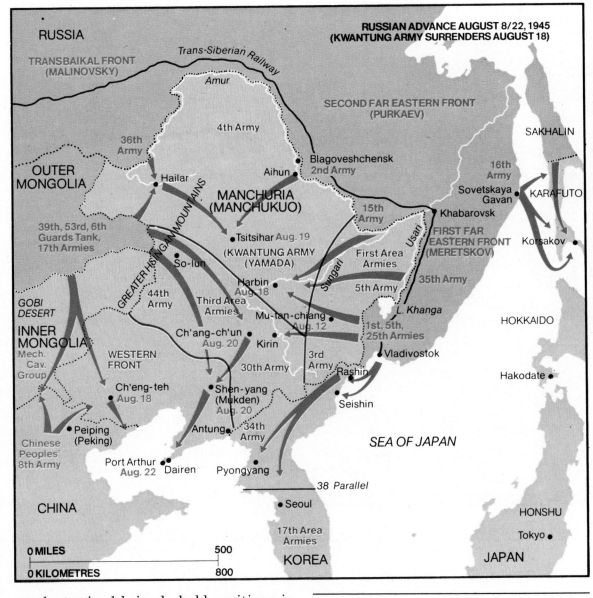

**RUSSIAN ADVANCE AUGUST 8/22, 1945
(KWANTUNG ARMY SURRENDERS AUGUST 18)**

RUSSIA

TRANSBAIKAL FRONT
(MALINOVSKY)

Trans-Siberian Railway

Amur

36th
Army

OUTER
MONGOLIA

Hailar

MANCHURIA
(MANCHUKUO)

4th Army

Aihun

Blagoveshchensk
2nd Army

SECOND FAR EASTERN FRONT
(PURKAEV)

SAKHALIN

16th
Army

Sovetskaya
Gavan

Khabarovsk

KARAFUTO

39th, 53rd, 6th
Guards Tank,
17th Armies

So-lun

Tsitsihar Aug. 19

(KWANTUNG ARMY)
(YAMADA)

15th
Army

First Area
Armies

FIRST FAR
EASTERN FRONT
(MERETSKOV)

Korsakov

GOBI
DESERT

INNER
MONGOLIA

Mech.
Cav.
Group

44th
Army

Third Area
Armies

Harbin
Aug. 18

Mu-tan-chiang
Aug. 12

5th Army

35th Army

Sungari

Usuri

HOKKAIDO

GREATER HSINGAN MOUNTAINS

WESTERN
FRONT

Ch'ang-ch'un
Aug. 20

Kirin

30th Army

L. Khanga

1st, 5th,
25th Armies

Ch'eng-teh
Aug. 18

Shen-yang
(Mukden)
Aug. 20

3rd
Army

Rashin

Vladivostok

Hakodate

Antung

34th
Army

Seishin

Chinese
Peoples'
8th Army

Peiping
(Peking)

SEA OF JAPAN

Port Arthur
Aug. 22

Dairen

Pyongyang

38 Parallel

CHINA

Seoul

HONSHU

0 MILES   500

17th Area
Armies

Tokyo

0 KILOMETRES   800

KOREA

JAPAN

◁ ◁ ◁ *Japanese prisoners in
Dunhua.*
◁ ◁ *A column of P.O.W.s
moves to its collecting point in
the Dunhua area. Many of the
men who made up the Japanese
Kwantung Army were unfit or
over-aged. The Russians,
however, used them as a pool of
free labour to work on their
industrial projects in the East.
Estimates of the Japanese
losses vary: their casualties were
between 20,000 and 80,000, and
among the 600,000 prisoners
were 148 generals.*
◁ *Blitzkrieg, Russian style, in
the Far East. The thrust across
the desert and mountains on the
western border of Manchuria
caught the Japanese unprepared
and achieved the deepest
penetrations.*

pendent mixed brigade held positions in
the Hailar area, a division and two independent mixed brigades were in the
Heiho–Sunwu area, and one division was
at Tsitsihar with a mixed brigade at
Harbin. The 119th Infantry Division,
which was at Hailar, was one of the best
units in the Kwantung Army, but even
then it was only rated 70 per cent effective.
In the same area the 80th Independent
Mixed Brigade was rated as the weakest
unit, at 15 per cent effectiveness.

Against this opposition the 6th Guards
Tank Army had been set a break-neck
timetable. Two days were allocated to
crossing the desert, making an average of
65 miles a day. During this move it was
expected to seize suitable sites for building
airstrips. Three days were allowed for
crossing the mountains, securing the
ridge, and moving down to the Lu-pei–
Li-chuan line, a distance of 50 miles a
day; then within five days it was to take
Mukden and Ch'ang-ch'un.

The war begins

On August 8, there were no rolling
barrages to announce the attack in the
east by the 6th Guards Tank Army, just the
roar of massed tank engines. There was no
need for any preparatory fire, for the army
met no opposition during the first four
days.

The northern axis was led by VII
Mechanised Corps, the southern by IX
Mechanised Corps, with V Guards Tank
Corps in the rear. The lack of opposition
changed this formation, and in a spectacular advance which at times reached 25
mph, each of the two mechanised corps
formed into six to eight parallel columns.

By the time they reached the Great
Hsingan range on August 10, IX Mechanised Corps was low on fuel. V Guards
Tank Corps moved up to make the crossing
during the night.

△ *Soviet Marines in an informal victory parade in Harbin. These men may be part of the Amur River Flotilla which entered the Sungari river and moved upwards to Harbin. The town was captured by an ad hoc* airborne *unit.*

The mountain road was a nightmare, with 30-degree turns and many defiles, and at places it had to be shored up by engineers. V Guards Tank Corps made the 25-mile crossing in seven hours. VII Mechanised Corps moved more slowly and completed it by the evening of August 11.

Over the mountains, the corps adopted battle formation, and with no roads, petrol and oil consumption increased. Behind the tanks the tail units bogged down in their trucks on the battered mountain roads. On August 10 the first fuel supplies were brought in by air.

By the end of August 11 advanced units of V Guards Tank Corps had taken Lu-pei, and on the 12th, VII Mechanised Corps had taken Li-chuan. As yet they had made no real contact with the enemy. The first phase had been completed on time.

But now the incomplete logistic preparation caught up. For two days they waited: V Guards Tank Corps' fuel tanks were just over half empty, VII Mechanised Corps' were half empty, while IX Mechanised Corps' had no fuel at all

left. Men as well as machines suffered; many had not had a hot meal for days.

Aircraft flew 2,072 tons of fuel and oil to the 6th Guards Tank Army and 384 tons to other units on the front during the operation. But the aircraft were not designed for heavy bulk cargoes and it needed 1,755 sorties to bring in the fuel.

In the north the 36th Army hit a fortified line near Man-chou-li, but this was soon overcome and the army advanced 25 miles in the first day. Hailar was by-passed and reduced slowly, falling on the 18th. It was a spectacular stand by the Japanese 80th Brigade which was attacked by the three rifle divisions and a tank brigade. The Japanese fought on, in ignorance of the capitulation on August 15.

The 39th Army also fought with units of the Japanese 107th Division, which had not heard of the surrender, and Wang-yeh-miao fell on the 21st. Though some 7,850 Japanese had surrendered by the 24th, some fought on until the end of August.

The 17th Army met no resistance crossing the Hsingan mountains and reached Dabanshan on August 15. Ironically the horsemen of the mixed Mongolian and Russian cavalry force did better than their mechanised comrades. By August 20 they had pushed over the border into China, leaving the tanks and armoured cars of the 17th Army stranded for lack of fuel.

On August 15 Marshal Malinovsky ordered the 6th Guards Tank Army and the 39th Army to give detachments of brigade strength the rôle that had previously been assigned to corps. These units were fully topped up with all the available fuel and ordered to press on with the advance. The rest of the corps would follow as fuel became available.

As it developed, smaller advanced reconnaissance units forged ahead and fulfilled the corps and army objectives. The Motorcycle Battalion of IX Mechanised Corps operated more than 100 miles ahead of the main force between August 14 and 17. V Guards Tank Corps' reconnaissance detachment took the bridge and airfield at T'ung-liao and VII Mechanised Corps' reconnaissance detachment took Taonan. Larger advanced units followed on August 16, but the main forces only arrived on the 18th.

Despite its surrender, the Kwantung Army continued to retreat and so Malinovsky ordered the 6th Guards Tank Army to take Ch'ang-ch'un and Mukden, and after leaving a reinforced brigade in each town, to proceed as quickly as possible to Port Arthur and other ports.

The 39th Army was ordered to liquidate the A-erh-shan pocket and move to Ch'ang-ch'un and Ssu-p'ing. The 36th Army was to mop up Hailar and move on to Tsitsihar, T'ai-lai, and An-kuang. The 53rd Army (Lieutenant-General I. M. Managarov) would fill the gap between the 6th Guards Tank Army and the 17th Army, and occupy K'ai-lu.

On August 18 a company-size force composed of engineers and some experienced airborne troops air-landed at Harbin. A day later 225 men landed at Mukden and 200 men at Ch'ang-ch'un; a landing was also made at Kirin. These operations were launched to prevent the escape to Japan of valuable prisoners and the destruction of equipment and stores.

On August 19, the 36th Army took Tsitsihar. A day later advanced units of V Guards Tank Corps occupied Mukden, on the 21st VII Mechanised Corps took Ch'ang-ch'un. Air landings were made at Port Arthur and Dairen by 250 men on August 22. Tanks from V Guards Tank Corps were loaded on railway flat cars and sent from Mukden to Port Arthur, where they arrived on the 24th.

From August 24 to 29 the main force of the 6th Guards Tank Army concentrated in Mukden, Dairen, and Port Arthur. It had moved over 700 miles and been halted only by lack of fuel.

The 12th Air Army had flown 2,361 combat missions and 3,167 reconnaissance and supply missions. Bombers had dropped a modest 710.7 tons of explosive. Ground forces had fired 14,746 shells and 42,134 bullets, according to Soviet sources.

The Japanese had made little contact with them as a result of a breakdown in communications, and because they had deployed their forces well back from the frontier.

1st Far Eastern Front

On the other side of Manchuria, the 1st Far Eastern Front went into action on August 8. Although it faced fixed defences, these were manned by the Japanese 1st Area Army (under General S. Kita), which included three divisions and one brigade formed from over-age reservists with less than one month's training. None of the divisions was fully equipped or had any combat experience, and the positions were short of artillery and ammunition.

The anti-tank defences were also incomplete.

In a night attack, in driving rain, the Soviet 5th Army (Colonel-General N. I. Krylov) and the 1st Red Banner Army (Lieutenant-General A. P. Beloborodov) stormed the border fortifications. They were supported by 320 guns per mile of front, and each division was allocated a front of two miles. There was a brief but savage battle and by the end of the day the Russians had advanced about $7\frac{1}{2}$ miles.

Hu-t'ou and Tung-ning fell within the first two days, and by August 11 Mu-leng and Hunchun had fallen. Some by-passed Japanese garrisons fought on until August 26. At Sui-fe-ho, fierce fighting lasted until August 10.

The key to the front was the town of Mu-tan-chiang, where the Japanese 5th Army (Lieutenant-General N. Shimizu) had concentrated. It was attacked from the air and LIX Rifle Corps and the 75th Tank Brigade of the 1st Army took Lin-k'ou and cut the town off from the north. While XXVI Rifle Corps and the 257th Tank Brigade tightened this grip from the

△ *Fraternisation with the natives: men of a Russian tank unit sample Chinese food in Dalny near Port Arthur. They are part of the Transbaikal Front, which had a gruelling timetable of towns and physical features to capture in the opening days of the campaign.*

north, the 5th Army ploughed ahead from the east. Fighting lasted from August 11 to 14, when XXVI Rifle Corps entered the town.

On the 15th the Japanese regained control of the town and their rear defence line, in a counter-attack that pushed XXVI Corps back six to eight miles to the north-east. It was only on the 16th that Soviet forces finally captured the town in the last major battle in the east.

When hostilities ceased, the 1st Area Army remained at about two-thirds of its effectiveness. Its 5th Army had sustained some heavy losses in the battle for Mu-tan-chiang, but the main forces were intact and falling back to the T'ung-hua redoubt according to plan.

In the Soviet 2nd Far Eastern Front, the smallest Russian forces faced the weakest enemy defences, for the Japanese had no plans to hold the salient of north-eastern Manchuria.

The Russians achieved an uncontested crossing of the Amur on August 9 and a day later the bulk of the 15th Army (Lieutenant-General S. K. Mamonov)

was shipped across. Men of the 361st Rifle Division moved over the Sungari and hit Fu-chin, where they encountered the Japanese 134th Infantry Division.

It was a hard fight lasting several days, and General Purkaev assumed personal command despite the fact that he was also responsible for the crossing at Blago-veshchensk and the landings on Sakhalin Island. Only on August 14 was the Japanese 134th Division forced to withdraw.

2nd Army advances

The crossings at Blagoveshchensk were made on the night of August 9–10. Again the crossing was easy, but later the Russians hit fierce resistance at Aihun, where the Japanese 135th Brigade continued to fight until it learned of the capitulation on August 19.

The island of Sakhalin had been divided almost equally between the Japanese and the Russians since 1905. The original

Soviet plans here had been to remain on the defensive, but following the initial successes in Manchuria, Marshal Vasilevsky decided to take the southern section in an amphibious and land attack.

There was a garrison of about 20,000 men in the south, but the Soviet forces outnumbered it in a ratio of 3.7 to 1 in infantry companies, 10 to 1 in artillery, and 4.3 to 1 in machine guns. The Russians had complete control of the air, and almost total control at sea.

Despite this, the Japanese put up a stiff resistance to the landings on August 11, made by the Soviet 79th Rifle Division. On August 14 they counter-attacked and cut off the 179th Regiment of the 79th Division.

Landings were made by marines at Maoka on August 19 in an attempt to outflank the Japanese defences, and on the 20th the defence began to crumble.

On the Kurile island chain there was almost parity in the strength of the opposing forces. Landings were made on Shumshu on August 18 but they were fiercely resisted by the Japanese. The capitulation came in time, however, to spare the Russians a real taste of what the Americans had experienced throughout the south Pacific.

In fact the Japanese capitulation came in time to spare all the Soviet forces in the Far East. Though the Transbaikal Front achieved a major victory, other fronts had encountered some characteristically fierce Japanese defensive fighting.

A measure of the cost of this fighting is reflected in the Russian ammunition expenditure (361,079 shells and 1,023,697 bullets) and their casualties, which are probably understated (8,219 killed and 22,264 wounded).

Estimates of Japanese losses vary; the Russians claim 83,737 killed and 594,000 prisoners, though unofficial and perhaps incomplete Japanese sources give 21,000 killed.

Weapons captured from the Japanese were made available to the Chinese Communist forces who used them in the Civil War, which ended in 1949. With its end, peace came to China after nearly 50 years of war.

△ *Soviet Marines cheer on the Golden Crag at Port Arthur. The capture of the former Imperial Russian port settled a long-standing account with the Japanese, who had captured it in the war of 1904-1905. Stalin himself commented that this was something "which we of the older generation had not forgotten".*

CHAPTER 178
Hiroshima

by Dr. Frank Futrell

Previous page: *The symbol of a new age, the mushroom cloud of an atomic explosion. J.R. Oppenheimer, one of the members of the development team at Oak Ridge, declared: "The physicists have known sin."*
△ *"Enola Gay", the B-29 which delivered the first atomic attack on Hiroshima.*
△▷ *The bomber's crew. Only Colonel Tibbets and Captain Parson (front row, 2nd and 3rd from right) knew the plane's destination.*
▷▷ *General L.R. Groves, the director of the "Manhattan Project". Under him was a team of brilliant and sometimes temperamental men whose work was so secret that even their wives thought they were part of a peaceful industrial establishment.*
△▷▷ *"Little Boy", the first atomic weapon. With a diameter of 28 inches, a length of 120 inches, and a weight of 900 lbs, the bomb had the power of 20,000 tons of T.N.T.*

By the spring of 1945 the ganglion of Government, Imperial Household, Army, and Navy rulers who made Japan's national policy in the name of Emperor Hirohito was struggling to end the disastrous war with a negotiated peace which hopefully would avoid Allied military occupation and, in all events, would preserve Japan's historic imperial system. Japan was clearly defeated: following failure to secure Russia's good offices for negotiations, the last hope for a conditional peace was the bitter proposal of the irrevocable Minister of War, General Korechika Anami, that Japan must fight to the end in defence of the home islands. Japan still had two million combat troops and 9,000 *kamikaze* aircraft. These forces could be expected to wreak tremendous casualties upon American invaders, who, in the end, would be compelled to negotiate a peace.

American assessments of the situation were not vastly different from those of General Anami. Japan was defeated, besieged from the sea, and was being pulverised by U.S. Navy carrier aircraft and by U.S. Army Air Forces B-29 bombers that were flying from bases in the Marianas. At a meeting in the White House on June 18, 1945, U.S. Army Chief-of-Staff General George C. Marshall urged that Japan must be invaded in order to end the war, and President Harry S Truman gave a go-ahead for planned landings on Kyushu on November 1, 1945 (Operation "Olympic"), and five months later against Honshu (Operation "Coronet"). While Marshall supported invasion, he was concerned about potential American casualties, estimating that 69,000 Americans would be killed or wounded in a 190,000-man operation against Kyushu. Japanese troops had amply demonstrated that they could and would fight desperately even when the outlook was hopeless.

One hope for enforcing a Japanese surrender, short of invasion, which was discussed at the White House on June 18, 1945, was a prediction of the highly secret U.S. Army Manhattan Engineer

District project that two atomic bombs would be available for operational employment by the end of July. The first of these revolutionary weapons would be the bomb called the "Little Boy", a gun-assembly weapon with an explosive Uranium-235 core—fissionable material that had been laboriously extracted at a giant Manhattan plant at Oak Ridge, Tennessee. Atomic scientists were confident that the gun principle would work, that an explosive charge would drive a plug of U-235 into the U-235 core, establishing a critical mass and an explosion of gigantic dimensions. The scientists were less confident that the other type of bomb could be made to function. This was the "Fat Man", and it was an implosion weapon which used plutonium (Pu-239) bred in nuclear reactors at Hanford, Washington. The implosion weapon principle would require testing in mid-July at a proving ground near Alamogordo, New Mexico: and, if the principle worked, a "Fat Man" would be available at the end of the month.

The United States Army Air Forces had already provided everything required to drop the atomic bombs when they were ready. The 509th Composite Group had been activated in December 1944 under the command of Colonel Paul W. Tibbets, Jr., and included the 393rd Bombardment Squadron with the most advanced model long-range B-29 bombers—the only American aircraft big enough to carry the first atomic weapons. The group had trained at Wendover, Utah, and in April-May 1945 had moved to North Field on Tinian Island in the Marianas. Both in training and in familiarisation flights to Japan, the 509th Group had been dropping orange-painted 10,000-pound T.N.T.-filled bombs (quite naturally called "Pumpkin

GROVES

bombs" because of their shape and colour), which were similar in ballistic characteristics to the "Fat Man". There was a derisive song being sung on Tinian to the effect that the 509th was going to win the war, but no one knew exactly how, since only Colonel Tibbets and a few others in the group shared the atomic secret. A target committee of Manhattan Project and Army Air Forces representatives had nominated the cities of Kokura, Hiroshima, Niigata, and Kyoto for the first atomic strikes, and afterward Nagasaki was substituted for Kyoto when Secretary of War Henry L. Stimson forbade an attack against Kyoto because of its cultural antiquities.

American military leaders understood Japan's reluctance to surrender her ancient *Tenno* or imperial system, and they also reasoned that the Emperor would be the only authority that could enforce a capitulation of Japan's military forces. The military leaders were therefore inclined to clarify the Allied unconditional surrender terms enough to permit Japan to retain her Emperor. This view was not accepted at the Allied heads of state "Terminal" conference in Potsdam. Instead, the Potsdam proclamation published on July 26 called for an unconditional surrender of all Japanese armed forces, or else acceptance of "prompt and utter destruction". In the assessment of historian Robert J. C. Butow, the absence of mention of the Emperor in the Potsdam proclamation was "an invaluable trump card" offered to the Japanese militarists, and on July 28 Prime Minister Kantaro Suzuki announced that his government would *mokusatsu* the proclamation–literally, "kill" it "with silence", or more idiomatically "treat it with silent contempt". Suzuki favoured peace and may well have used the wrong word, but the response unleashed violent reactions.

Events moved swiftly, and President Truman had learned of the world's first nuclear detonation at its occurrence at Alamogordo on July 16. The implosion principle–whereby a core of plutonium was wrapped with T.N.T. blocks which when detonated simultaneously squeezed the core into a critical mass–had worked, and the "Fat Man" was practicable. In Washington, General Carl A. Spaatz, on his way to take command of the United States Army Strategic Air Forces in the Pacific, was told of the atomic strike plans, and, after refusing to drop such bombs on oral directions, received written orders that the 509th Group would deliver its first "special bomb" as soon after about August 3 as weather would permit a visual attack against Hiroshima, Kokura, Niigata, or Nagasaki. The first bomb would be the reliable "Little Boy". The U.S. cruiser *Indianapolis* delivered most of the U-235 needed to arm it at Tinian on July 26 and headed on toward the Philippines. (Four days later it was sunk in mid-ocean by Japanese submarine torpedoes.) On August 2, the 20th Air Force mimeographed top secret operations orders for Special Bombing Mission No. 13; the primary target was Hiroshima, with Kokura the secondary and Nagasaki the tertiary. Since visual bombing was mandatory, an advance B-29 weather observer aircraft would scout and report on each target. The strike mission included an atomic laden B-29 and two observer B-29's.

Predictions of bad weather over southern Japan held off the attack until August 6, 1945, when at 0245 hours Colonel Tibbets lifted his B-29, named the "Enola Gay" after his mother, off the runway at North Field and was followed at two minute intervals by the observer planes. At take-off the "Enola Gay" grossed 65 tons in weight, eight tons over normal B-29 bombing weight, partly because of the fact that the "Little Boy" weighed 9,000 pounds. Since a crash of the plane while taking off might have blown one end off Tinian Island, Captain William S. ("Deac") Parsons, a U.S. Navy ordnance expert who accompanied Tibbets as weaponeer and bomb commander, armed the "Little Boy" during the flight toward Japan.

Hiroshima dies

At 0715 hours on August 6, 1945, the weather scout B-29 over Hiroshima piloted by Major Claude Eatherly signalled that the target was open, thus sealing the fate of the city. As the weather

△ *The devastation at Hiroshima. Sixty per cent of the city had been destroyed, with 86,000 inhabitants killed and 61,000 injured. On the right is the domed Agricultural Exhibition Hall which remains today as a ruin, a memorial for the first victim of an atomic attack.*

plane departed, the Hiroshima all-clear air defence signal was sounded at 0731. Until now the city had almost entirely escaped air attack, and few people took the appearance of a few high-flying planes seriously. Thus sightings at 0806 of two B-29's with a third in trail, all flying very high at an altitude of 31,600 feet, did not seem significant enough to call another defence alert. But those Japanese who watched the approaching planes (and who survived) noticed that the lead bombers suddenly separated in tight diving turns that carried them rapidly away from a point in space where something fell from the planes–the "Little Boy" from the "Enola Gay" and parachuted instruments from the observation plane. Exactly 17 seconds after 0815 hours an instant of pure, blinding, utterly intense bluish-white light cut across the sky, followed by searing heat, a thousand-fold crash of thunder, and finally an earth-shaking blast that sent a mushroom cloud of dust and debris boiling up to 50,000 feet. This was the moment that survivors at Hiroshima would remember as the *pikadon*–the *pika* or "flash" followed by the *don* or "thunder".

As a military objective, the city of Hiroshima was chiefly important as a port and the site of an army garrison. Located on seven finger-like deltaic islands where the mouth of the Ota river pushes out from the underside of Honshu into the Inland Sea, Hiroshima had been the point of embarkation for Japanese troops moving into China and to the South Seas. It was also the seat of the 2nd General Army, which was responsible for defence of the south-western section of the homeland. Volunteer and government-enforced evacuations had reduced the city's

population from 380,000 in 1942 to about 255,200 in 1945, but it remained Japan's seventh largest city.

The "Little Boy" was aimed at a bridge in almost the centre of the built-up part of the city, and it detonated at an altitude of just below 2,000 feet, almost precisely on its mark, with a force later calculated to have been equivalent to 17,000 tons (or 17 kilotons) of T.N.T. By blast and by an ensuing firestorm, approximately 4.7 square miles around the ground zero (directly below the bomb burst) were completely destroyed. Approximately 60,000 out of 90,000 buildings within 9.5 square miles were destroyed or badly damaged. Very few people had taken shelter, and the full extent of personnel casualties at Hiroshima will never be known. The Japanese eventually inscribed the names of 61,443 known dead on the cenotaph erected at ground zero. On the other hand, the United States Strategic Bombing Survey estimated that there were 139,402 casualties, including 71,379 known dead and missing (presumed to be dead) and 68,023 injured, of whom 19,691 were known to be seriously injured. The Bombing Survey estimated that over 20,000 of the killed and missing were school children. Ironically for a strategic bombing attack, most of Hiroshima's larger industrial factories were on the perimeter of the city, and these factories (and the workers who had already reported for duty) escaped destruction. The Bombing Survey concluded that only 26 per cent of Hiroshima's total production plant was destroyed in the atomic strike and that the plants could have been kept in operation if the war had continued.

Nagasaki's turn

Where the execution of the "Enola Gay" mission against Hiroshima was almost flawless and all crews returned immediately to Tinian, the 509th Composite Group's second mission, flown on August 9 with the more efficient "Fat Man" plutonium bomb, went much less smoothly. Again there were to be three planes in the striking force, an armed B-29 called "Bock's Car" piloted by Major Charles W. Sweeney and two observer aircraft. The city of Niigata was ruled out as too far distant for attack, leaving Kokura as the primary target and Nagasaki as the alternative. Kokura was

△ *A Japanese civilian caught in the flash of the atomic explosion. The bright light has burned his skin in the pattern of the kimono he was wearing at the time of the attack. Many people who looked at the light which was "brighter than a thousand suns" were permanently blinded.*

important because it was the location of a vast army arsenal on the northern tip of Kyushu. Nagasaki had a fine harbour of some commercial importance and four large Mitsubishi war production industrial plants. Unlike Hiroshima's flat deltaic terrain, Nagasaki's topography was broken by hills and valleys, which promised to reduce destruction. Both Kokura and Nagasaki were to be scouted in advance by weather B-29's. Prediction of weather over Kyushu dictated that the strike mission had to be flown on August 9, and since a storm was building up *en route* to Japan the strike B-29 and the two observer planes to accompany it were scheduled to fly northward individually and rendezvous over Yakoshima Island off the south coast of Kyushu before proceeding to their target.

There was considerable apprehension on Tinian as Major Sweeney launched the "Bock's Car" from North Field at 0349 hours on August 9. Another U.S. Navy ordnance expert, Commander Frederick L. Ashworth, was aboard as bomb commander and weaponeer, but the 10,000-pound "Fat Man" had to be armed before take-off, greatly increasing the hazard of an atomic accident. Major Sweeney also discovered that 600 gallons of gasoline could not be pumped from an auxiliary tank in his plane, and this substantially reduced his reserve fuel supply. Sweeney lost additional time and fuel circling Yakoshima Island awaiting one of the observer B-29's, and after 40 minutes he decided to go on without it. (This aircraft, which happened to carry the official British observers, scientist William Penney and Group-Captain Leonard Cheshire, would arrive at the target a few minutes after the blast.) Apparently during the delay, clouds closed over Kokura, and after three runs over the city had failed to permit visual observation of the aiming point (but used up about 45 minutes additional time), the "Bock's Car" strike plane was headed for Nagasaki. It too was hidden by clouds; and in the emergency, with fuel steadily dwindling, Commander Ashworth authorised a radar drop. At the last moment a hole in the clouds permitted the bomb to be visually aimed and dropped at 1101 hours, but the "Fat Man" nevertheless missed the assigned aiming point by about three miles, a distance which placed the bomb over Nagasaki's industrial section rather than in its built-up commercial area.

After the drop, Major Sweeney headed to an emergency landing on Okinawa, where he landed with only a few gallons of fuel left.

Only vague references to an "incendiary" attack at Hiroshima had appeared in Japanese newspapers, and the people at Nagasaki were little prepared for the atomic strike. The weather B-29 had touched off an air raid alert at 0748, but nothing had happened, and at 1101 only about 400 people were in the city's tunnel shelters, which could have accommodated a third of Nagasaki's 195,290 registered inhabitants. As at Hiroshima, the "Fat Man" at Nagasaki was detonated in the air and at an altitude of approximately 1,750 feet. Where the atomic scientists had estimated that the magnitude of the plutonium bomb blast would range from 700 to 5,000 tons of T.N.T., the implosion principle of the "Fat Man" was much more efficient than that of the gun-type weapon, and the force of the "Fat Man" was estimated at 20 kilotons. With the more powerful bomb, and surrounding hills concentrating the blast, the scale of destruction at Nagasaki was greater than at Hiroshima, but the area destroyed and personnel casualties were smaller because terrain afforded protection from radiant heat and ionizing radiations to about one-fourth of the population. The area of greatest destruction was oval-shaped inside the narrow Urakami valley, approximately 1.45 square miles in size, and intervening hills saved the central part of the city from destruction. (By comparison, in Hiroshima approximately 60 per cent of the population was within 1.2 miles of the centre of the explosion; and in Nagasaki only 30 per cent of the population was so situated.) Official Japanese casualty figures nevertheless include 23,753 killed, 1,927 missing, and 23,345 injured, and these statistics number only verified cases. The United States Strategic Bombing Survey believed that the casualties were actually in the order of 35,000 dead and somewhat more than that injured. There was no fire storm at Nagasaki and less public panic. Since several of the large factories were in the area of maximum destruction, damage to industry in the Nagasaki strike was quite heavy; excluding the dockyard area (outside the radius of the bomb's effect) 68.3 per cent of the industrial productive area of the city was destroyed.

After a detailed investigation of Japan's struggle to end the war, the United States

Strategic Bombing Survey concluded that "certainly prior to 31 December 1945, and in all probability prior to 1 November 1945, Japan would have surrendered even if the atomic bombs had not been dropped, even if Russia had not entered the war, and even if no invasion had been planned or contemplated." On the other hand, the atomic attack doubtless hastened the Soviet Union's belated declaration of war upon Japan on August 8, and it certainly provided a powerful catalyst which enabled Japan's peace leaders to bring about a surrender over the continuing objections of War Minister Anami and the Army and Navy chiefs-of-staff. After Hiroshima the Japanese militarists attempted alternately to obscure the nature of the nuclear explosion and argued privately that the United States could not possibly possess enough radioactive material to permit a continuation of such attacks. The effect of these arguments failed with the Nagasaki strike, and in a hurriedly-called Imperial Conference on the night of August 9, 1945 Emperor Hirohito–the god figure who had never before been able to act without a consensus of his advisers–bluntly told the militarists that "to continue the war means nothing but the destruction of the whole nation" and that "the time has come when we must bear the unbearable". By the early morning hours of August 10, cables were on their way to Japan's diplomatic representatives in Berne and Stockholm announcing the nation's acceptance of the Potsdam ultimatum, with the sole proviso that the *Tenno* system would be preserved. This was to be the acceptable condition for the war's end when it came officially on September 2.

A-bombing: the after-effects

In plans for the atomic strikes, Manhattan Engineer District scientists were knowledgeable about the potential effects of radiation emitted from nuclear explosions, although the exact effect of nuclear radiation on human tissue was, and continues to be, incompletely explored. Nuclear radiation consists of alpha and beta particles and gamma rays, the latter being of great significance because of their long range and high penetrating character. It was expected that the air

bursts called for over the Japanese cities would limit casualties for the most part to non-radioactive injuries; namely, those due to the force and the heat of the unprecedented explosions. But when the final results were known, it was apparent from the experience at Hiroshima and Nagasaki that even without the effects of blast and fire the number of deaths among people within a radius of one-half mile from ground zero would have been almost as great as the actual figures, and deaths among those within one mile would have been only slightly less than they were. The cause was radiation sickness, which the Japanese called *genshibaku-dansho,* or the "sickness of the original-child bomb", among the *hibak'sha,* the "people who received the bomb".

According to the Japanese, individuals very near to the centre of the atomic explosions, but who escaped flash burns or secondary injuries, died rather quickly, the majority within a week, autopsies showing almost complete absence of white blood cells and deterioration of bone marrow. Most radiation cases, who were at greater distances, did not show severe symptoms for a week to a month after the bombs, when sudden high fevers marked the often-fatal onset of radiation sickness, again with dwindling white blood cell counts and disappearing bone marrow. The degree of the fever and the chance of survival bore a direct relation to the degree of exposure to radiation. Sperm counts done at Hiroshima revealed low counts or complete aspermia for as long as three months afterward among males who were within 5,000 feet of the

◁ *An atomic explosion in New Mexico. Observers were nearly ten miles from the explosion, and even here they wore welder's dark glasses against the fierce flash. Though the blast and flash of an atomic weapon seemed immediately awesome to victims and observers alike, the effects of radiation were an insidious by-product of the bomb which lingered long after the war.*
△ *Survivors of Hiroshima leave the devastated city. In the background a building burns, after being caught in the fierce flash of the explosion.*

centre of the explosion. Two months after the explosion, Hiroshima's total incidence of miscarriages, abortions, and premature births was 27 per cent as compared with a normal rate of six per cent.

At both Hiroshima and Nagasaki immediate deaths from radiation peaked in three to four weeks and practically ceased after seven to eight weeks. Both Hiroshima and Nagasaki were rebuilt and regained prosperity, the prosperity ironically initially incidental to defence production undertaken for the United States military forces during the Korean War. As for the *hibak'sha*, the atomic casualty lists were never closed, since persons originally exposed have continued to die, apparently–although not completely conclusively–before their time. Fifteen years after the *pikadon*, for

example, Japanese physicians began to find abnormal incidence of thyroid cancer in people who were young children at the time of the bomb, and there has been an identified higher incidence of eye cataracts and leukaemia among the survivors of the A-bomb. The social trauma of keloid burn scars borne by many men and women immobilised these survivors in varying degrees. Many of these burn victims have expressed a belief that they have been discriminated against in gainful employment because of their disfigurements. Although children conceived by irradiated parents have appeared quite normal, some scientists continue to fear that one or two more generations born of atomic survivors must mature before the possibility of genetic mutations resulting from one day's exposure to gamma rays can be measured.

In a retrospective look at the A-bomb strikes, Lieutenant-General Leslie R. Groves, war-time director of the U.S. Army Manhattan District, has summed up the American belief about the matter: "The atomic bombings of Hiroshima and Nagasaki ended World War II. There can be no doubt of that. While they brought death and destruction on a horrifying scale, they averted even greater losses—American, English, and Japanese."

On the other side, the taped Japanese description of the bombing that may be heard in the Peace Memorial Museum in Hiroshima is more ambiguous, for here it is said: "When the Pacific War was finally about to end, at the stage where only a decisive battle on the mainland remained, the sudden disastrous event of Hiroshima was truly unfortunate to the people of Hiroshima, Japan and the whole world."

◁ *A lone survivor in the remains of Nagasaki, the city which was victim of "Fat Man", the second A-bomb, 132 inches long and 60 inches wide.*
▽ *Hiroshima. The report from U.S. Secretary of War Henry L. Stimson stated: "Results clear cut successful in all respects. Visible effects greater than in any test. Conditions normal in aircraft following delivery." On the ground people were roasted, vaporised, or subjected to massive doses of radiation which killed or crippled them, leaving slow-healing open wounds which remained as deep scars of rubbery pink tissue.*

CHAPTER 179

Japan surrenders

by Lawson Nagel

△ *General Numata and his party arrive from Saigon, on August 26, for the signing of the preliminary agreement for the surrender of all forces in South East Asia.*

△▷ *Elderly Japanese kneel and weep before the Imperial Palace in Tokyo following the surrender proclamation by Hirohito.*

△▷▷ *On board the* Missouri *in Tokyo Bay during the surrender ceremony on September 2, 1945.*

△▷▷▷ *A group of Japanese Kempetei (secret police) lay down their swords.*

▷ *The surrender signatories aboard the* Missouri. *They are (in the front row) Minister Mamoru Shigemitsu, to sign for the Emperor, and General Yoshijiro Umezu for the Japanese General Headquarters. In the second row (in top hats) are Katauo Okazaki and Toshikazu Kase, with other service and government representatives behind.*

In May 1945, the Japanese Army high command was despondent. Germany had surrendered, and it was obvious that the British and Americans were planning to redeploy their military strength for a final assault on the Japanese homeland. Relations with the Soviet Union had grown steadily worse, and there were fears that the Soviets might break their non-aggression pact with Japan and join the Western Allies. The Americans had recently captured Okinawa, only 400 miles from Japan, making it even easier than before for the American bombers to wreak havoc on Japanese cities.

Haunted by the spectre of Allied invasion of the homeland, some members of the high command privately suggested that it was time to consider negotiations. The Navy had admitted in October 1944 that it no longer had enough strength to launch an offensive. In December of the same year, the Americans had completed the Leyte campaign in the Philippines – a campaign which the Japanese premier had said would be decisive. From a strategic standpoint, Japan had already lost the war. Should not the nation surrender now, while retaining some strength and bargaining power, rather than risk total destruction in the invasion?

These fears were not shared by the majority of the high command in May 1945. They agreed that diplomatic attempts to keep the Soviet Union out of the war should be stepped up, but they expressed confidence that any Anglo-American invasion of the Japanese homeland could be repulsed. The main strength of the Army remained intact, and Japan's air force had been dispersed to many airfields to preserve it from destruction by American bombers. Plans to repulse the invaders called for the entire air force to attack the American transports and task forces in waves of *kamikaze* assaults. Army operations would be concentrated on the elimination of the invaders at their debarkation sites. If these operations were not successful, Japanese volunteer reserves would continue operations further inland. Above all, Army leaders said, "what should be remembered in carrying out the general decisive battle is adherence to a vigorous spirit of attack"

to "set the example for 100,000,000 compatriots". The high command felt that a single invasion could be defeated, although they held out no such hope of victory if the Americans launched second or third assaults in quick succession.

Emperor Hirohito himself was soon convinced that it would be necessary to negotiate. His civilian advisers told him that the military situation was hopeless and the war must be ended immediately. Early in July 1945, therefore, while the high command was planning to repulse the invaders and fight to the last man, the diplomats were appealing to the Soviet Union to act as mediator in order to end the war.

The Potsdam Declaration

On July 17, Stalin met with Truman and Churchill at Potsdam. He informed the Western leaders that the Japanese had approached him about peace talks, but seemed unprepared to accept the Allies' demand for unconditional surrender. Truman and Churchill, along with Chiang Kai-shek, issued the Potsdam Proclamation on July 26, reiterating the demand that surrender be unconditional. Otherwise, the proclamation declared, Japan would face "prompt and utter destruction". It did not state that this destruction would be brought about by a new weapon – the atomic bomb.

The debate in top Japanese diplomatic and military circles now revolved around the meaning of the word "unconditional". Did this mean that the nation must surrender, as well as the armed forces? Did it mean that the Emperor would be deposed and the Imperial institution abolished? The Potsdam Proclamation had been silent on this point. Both the diplomats and the high command were determined to support the Emperor, and the generals knew that their men would never accept any agreement which abolished the Imperial institution. In the words of one high-ranking officer, "it would be useless for the people to survive the war if the structure of the State itself were to be destroyed. . . . even if the whole Japanese race were all but wiped out, its determination to preserve the national policy would be forever recorded in the annals of history, but a people who sacrificed will upon the altar of physical existence could never rise again as a nation."

In the midst of this debate, on August 6, the first atomic bomb was dropped on Hiroshima. Three days later a second atomic bomb devastated Nagasaki, and the Soviet Union finally declared war on Japan. A conference of the Emperor and his civilian and military advisers was hastily summoned, and met in an air-raid shelter in the grounds of the Imperial Palace in Tokyo shortly before midnight. In the light of the events of the past three days, even the military authorities agreed now that a surrender was unavoidable. Unlike Foreign Minister Togo, however, who advised surrender on the single condition that the Emperor's rights be preserved, the military leaders asked for three other reservations. First, they wanted to avoid an Allied military occupation of Japan. Second, they wanted to try war criminals themselves. Third, they wanted to disarm their own troops rather than surrender directly to the Allies. War Minister Anami explained that this last proviso could be taken to mean that the Japanese armed forces were not actually defeated, but had decided to stop fighting voluntarily in order to preserve the Japanese land and people from further destruction. When

△ *General Takazo Numata surrenders in Rangoon.*
▽ *British proclamations are displayed in Saigon.*

PROCLAMATION Nº 1

PROCLAMATION No 1

I. — With the unconditional surrender to the Allied Nations by all Japanese forces, signed in the name of the Emperor of Japan at Tokyo on 2nd September 1945, the Supreme Allied Commander of all Allied Forces in South East Asia Command, Admiral Lord Louis Mountbatten, G. C. V. O., K. C. B., D. S. O., has delegated to me, General D. D. Gracey C. B., C. B. E., M. C., the command of all British, French and Japanese forces and of all police forces and other armed bodies in French Indo China South of 16° latitude, with orders to ensure law and order in this area.

II. — Let it be known to all, that it is my firm intention to ensure with strict impartiality that this period of transition from war to peace conditions is carried out peaceably, with the minimum dislocation to all public and utility services, legitimate businesses and trade, and with the least interference with the normal peaceful activities and avocations of the people.

III. — I call on all citizens in the name of the Supreme Allied Commander to co-operate to the fullest extent to achieve the above object, and hereby warn all wrong doers, especially looters and saboteurs of public and private property, and those also carrying out similar criminal activities, that they will be summarily shot

IV. — The following orders will come into immediate effect:
a/ No demonstrations or processions will be permitted.
b/ No public meetings will take place.
c/ No arms of any description including sticks, staves, bamboo spears etc., will be carried except by British and Allied troops, and such other forces and police which have been specially authorised by me.
d/ The curfew already imposed on my orders by the Japanese authorities between 21:30 and 05:30 hrs in Saigon and Cholon, will be continued and strictly enforced.

Signed: D. D. GRACEY
Major-General, Comd. Allied Forces in Southern Indo China

REMOVAL OR DEFACEMENT OF THIS PROCLAMATION IS PROHIBITED

the two sides had expressed their views, the conference was found to be deadlocked. Then the unprecedented happened. The Emperor's advisers actually asked him for his own opinion. Instead of acting according to his advisers' instructions, the Emperor was being asked to advise them. He was to shed the rôle of observer and puppet and make his own decision. Hirohito had already made up his mind, and he soon made it clear that he believed the Foreign Minister's proposal – with only the Emperor's position safeguarded – was more likely to lead to a quick peace settlement and should therefore be accepted. The conference unanimously endorsed the Emperor's decision, and cables were sent within a few hours announcing the Japanese terms.

Hirohito steps in

Later that same day, a reply was received from U.S. Secretary of State James Byrnes. This note explained that the Allies would not accept anything but an unconditional surrender, and that this meant that the Emperor would be subject to the Supreme Commander for the Allied powers. This statement produced another argument in the Japanese cabinet – what did "subject to" mean? At another meeting on the morning of August 14, it was pointed out that Byrnes' note indicated that the Imperial institution would not be abolished, and in any case the Japanese Emperors had often been "subject to" the power of the *shoguns*. Once again, Hirohito was asked for his own opinion, and once again he called for immediate acceptance of the Allied demand. The cabinet acceded to the Imperial will, and it was announced over the radio that Japan had surrendered.

That night, the Emperor recorded a message to be broadcast at noon on August 15, calling for all Japanese to accept the surrender. They were warned especially to "beware strictly of any outbursts of emotion" that might create needless complications. In other words, they were to ignore any violent "fight-

△ *The Union Jack flies over Singapore.*
▽ *A Japanese officer surrenders his sword and salutes the colours.*

to-the-finish" fanatics. But a small group of officers at the Army headquarters were determined not to surrender, and decided to attempt a *coup d'état*. The Emperor was to be separated from his peace-seeking advisers and persuaded to change his mind and continue the war. On the night of August 14, the conspirators approached General Mori, the commander of the Imperial Guards, at the palace. They asked him to join with them in the *coup* to preserve the honour of the Japanese nation. Mori listened to their arguments, then said that he would go to pray at the Meiji Shrine to help him make up his mind. The conspirators were unwilling to allow any delay, and one of them shot Mori on the spot. Then, using the dead general's seal, they forged orders for the Imperial Guards and began tracking down the Emperor's advisers and the record which was to be broadcast the following day. The whole plot ended in failure when the Eastern Army District

commander arrived at the palace, refused to join the rebels, and persuaded them to give up. The officer who had shot General Mori committed *hara-kiri* on the Imperial Plaza. When War Minister Anami heard of the attempted *coup* early in the morning of August 15, he also committed suicide.

In the next few days, several other suicides occurred, but most Japanese accepted the Imperial decision calmly. On August 30, the first American occupation forces (including a small British contingent) landed at Yokosuka. Three days later, at nine o'clock in the morning, Japan's new Foreign Minister, Mamoru Shigemitsu, boarded the *Missouri* in Tokyo Bay. On behalf of the Emperor and the Japanese Government, he signed the official surrender document. General Douglas MacArthur accepted the surrender, a scratchy record of *The Star-Spangled Banner* was played on the ship's speakers, and World War II was over.

▽ *General of the Army Douglas MacArthur, Supreme Commander for the Allied Powers, signs the surrender document. Behind him are Lieutenant-General Jonathan Wainwright, who surrendered at Corregidor, and Lieutenant-General A.E. Percival, who surrendered at Singapore. They attended the ceremonies on the* Missouri *at the personal invitation of General MacArthur.*

CHAPTER 180
Japan in defeat

by Richard Storry

For the overwhelming majority of the Japanese people, it was not so much national defeat as the unconditional capitulation of their armed forces, required by the Potsdam Declaration, that came as a totally unexpected, virtually unimaginable, bolt from the blue. For the survivors of Hiroshima and Nagasaki the Emperor's surrender broadcast on August 15, 1945 was a more devastating psychological shock than the atomic bombs.

The mood throughout Japan in the command to the nation to lay down its arms. Fanatics of this kind might claim that his broadcast did not represent his true feelings, that his words had been put into his mouth by traitors and faint hearts in the government and supreme command.

In fact, the instances of disobedience, though dramatic, were surprisingly few. On the night of August 14-15 there had been an abortive attempt by a group of young officers to prevent the surrender broadcast taking place. It was known that

◁ *James Morris's watercolour of the gutted remains of the Imperial Japanese Headquarters in Tokyo. The building was more than the hub of Japanese military strategy—because of Japan's constitution it was also the heart of political activity.*

aftermath of defeat was one of numbness and exhaustion mingled, as the days went by, with a sense of relief, an awareness of a providential escape from almost certain annihilation. There was also great uncertainty about the future. How would the occupying forces conduct themselves? Would there be attacks on lives and property? What kind of vengeance would the American troops exact? People fled from the larger cities and took refuge with relatives in the countryside. Nobody knew what to expect.

The Japanese Government, for its part, was worried primarily about the possibility of breaches of the peace by irreconcilable die-hards, superpatriots who might refuse to accept the Emperor's

the Emperor had recorded the broadcast on the evening of August 14; and as one of the insurgent officers put it:-

"We decided that the peace faction should be overruled and a *coup d'état* staged in order to prevail upon the Emperor to revoke his decision. The purpose of the projected *coup d'état* was to separate the Emperor from his peace-seeking advisers and persuade him to change his mind and continue the war."

The first aim of the insurgents was to destroy the recording of the Emperor's speech. This was hidden in the Imperial palace; but although the rebel officers had the palace grounds in their power they failed to discover the recording. The *coup* collapsed before dawn on August 15, thanks to the intervention of the local army commander.

In the centre of Tokyo a band of extremists seized Atago hill. The police handled the situation with caution, waiting a week before mounting their assault, whereupon the desperadoes killed themselves with hand grenades. Two days after the Emperor's broadcast some signals troops from a town north of Tokyo entered the capital and took possession of the Ueno art gallery. This was soon dealt with by loyal troops. The officers involved committed suicide, and the survivors returned to their barracks. From Atsugi airfield near Yokohama navy fliers dropped leaflets on Tokyo. These declared the surrender broadcast to be the work of

△ *The U.S. victors parade past General MacArthur's headquarters in the Dai Ichi Life Insurance building. Despite the Americans' massive presence, the worst Japanese fears about them were soon put to rest.*

traitors. This instance of insubordination was quickly put down. It was a particular source of anxiety to the government, since Atsugi had been designated as the airfield at which the first occupying troops would land later in the month.

Elsewhere, apart from one or two isolated incidents, things were quiet; although on August 14, when hostilities were supposed to have ceased, the commander of the 5th Navy Air Fleet led an unauthorised sortie from Kyūshū against enemy shipping in the Okinawa area. None of the 11 planes returned.

More impressive even than the general acceptance of the surrender in the home islands was the remarkable *volte-face*, from fierce antagonism to co-operation

with the enemy's demands, on the part of the 3,300,000 Japanese fighting men distributed over the huge area that stretched from Korea and Manchuria to the islands of the South Seas. The great armies in China, for example, regarded themselves as unbeaten, perhaps unbeatable; and there were a great many formations—in much of Indonesia, in Thailand, Malaya, and French Indo-China, in the Pacific—which had not been in action for a considerable time. They were in a sense fresh, confident, and eager for battle. But they obeyed the call from Tokyo to comply with the will of the enemy—as did the Japanese forces locked in combat with the Russians in Manchuria, Korea, and Sakhalin. The same applied to the Japanese soldiers in Burma, Borneo, New Guinea, and the Philippines. It was striking proof of the final authority of the Imperial house. Thorough indoctrination at home, at school, and in military training camps, had led the Japanese to fight literally to the death—to the last man in many a hopeless battle—on Iwo Jima and Okinawa and in the Manchurian plain, not to mention the jungles of New Guinea, the Solomons, the Philippines, and Burma. Now the same indoctrination, compelling respect for the Emperor's will, enabled them to accept the unacceptable, or (in the Emperor's own words) "to bear the unbearable".

In accordance with that injunction, few national leaders took their own lives, to atone for their failure to avert defeat. But Vice-Admiral Ohnishi, founder of the *kamikaze* squadrons, Lieutenant-General Anami, Minister of War, and Field-Marshal Sugiyama, commander of the 1st Army, committed suicide. One or two other senior officers at home and abroad followed the same road. Later, General Tojo tried to kill himself when he learned he was to be arrested as a suspected war criminal. In much the same circumstances another former Prime Minister, Prince Konoye, took a lethal dose of poison. But such cases were exceptional. On the whole, public men swallowed the bitterness of defeat and surrender, largely from respect for the Emperor who was ready himself to "bear the unbearable".

In the interval of about two weeks between the Japanese surrender and the arrival of the Americans, there was considerable destruction of confidential documents at various ministries in Tokyo and the general staff headquarters of the armed services. There was also a new cabinet, headed by the Emperor's cousin, Prince Higashi-Kuni. Its main preoccupation, as we have noted, was the control of public order and, so far as this was feasible, the maintenance of national morale.

The occupying forces started to arrive in the early hours of August 28. To the relief of all concerned, no untoward incidents occurred. The advance party of Americans was driven in Japanese lorries from Atsugi airfield, littered with the wreckage of navy planes, to the devastated city of Yokohama, designated as the headquarters of the U.S. 8th Army. There were few spectators. At every intersection on the route a Japanese soldier, his rifle and bayonet at the ready, stood with his back to the convoy, on guard against any possible surprise attack on the Americans. It was a silent and dismal scene.

Within the next four days large forces had landed not only at Atsugi but also at various seaports; and the U.S. 3rd Fleet, with the British Pacific Fleet, lay at anchor in Tokyo Bay. General Mac-Arthur himself arrived at Atsugi in his special plane, "Bataan". The stage was set for the formal act of surrender on September 2.

At this juncture the Japanese won a concession from the Americans, although it proved to be as advantageous to the latter as to the Japanese. A ministerial delegation from Tokyo waited upon Mac-Arthur at Yokohama after his arrival and persuaded him of the practicability of governing Japan through the established Japanese administrative organs rather than by direct military rule, as in Occupied Germany. Thus the occupation of Japan was not in a strict sense a "military government". The several departments of S.C.A.P. (Supreme Commander for the Allied Powers) were overlords supervising and working through the corresponding departments of the Japanese Government. But they were overlords whose will was not to be evaded, much less defied, and in fact a very notable feature of the occupation was the way in which Japanese officials at all levels co-operated.

Surrender on board

The surrender ceremony took place on the American battleship *Missouri*. The Japanese Foreign Minister, Mamoru Shigemitsu, signed on behalf of the government. General Umezu, Chief of the Army General Staff, signed for the supreme command. The small Japanese party was in formal dress, the civilians in top hats and morning coats. Slender to the point of emaciation, the Japanese presented a contrast with the well-fed American generals and admirals lined up on the deck in khaki drill slacks and open-neck shirts. Above them, standing on the turrets, and perched along the barrels of the 16-inch guns, were the crew of the *Missouri*. Later one of the Japanese– Shigemitsu's Foreign Ministry aide–was to record that for him the worst ordeal was the awareness of all the alien, watching eyes, that seemed to bore into his very soul. When the last signature had been inscribed (including those of Perci-

val, the British commander at the fall of Singapore, and Wainwright, the American commander at the fall of Corregidor) MacArthur stepped forward, declaring, in the vibrant tones characteristic of him: "Let us pray that peace be now restored to the world and that God will preserve it always. These proceedings are now closed."

The nation which the Americans–with some help from Britain and certain countries of the Commonwealth–proceeded to occupy was in a state of economic collapse and moral confusion. Only two or three cities of any size, among them Kyoto, had escaped punishment from the air. The gigantic urban complex of Tokyo-Kawasaki-Yokohama comprised 142 square

△ *Still wearing their uniforms, demobilised Japanese soldiers shop for food. Most necessities were in short supply, partly because of the disruption caused by American bombing, but also because the majority of farmers and fishermen had been called up to prepare for the defence of the home islands.*

3027

miles, of which no less than 70 square miles were completely flattened and burnt out. From a total of 1,454,000 buildings nearly 863,000 had been destroyed. Approximately eight million people had inhabited the area, and of these 3.4 million had lost their homes. Ashes, charred wood, and rubble were all that could be seen over the 16 miles or more from the docks of Yokohama to the Marunouchi district of Tokyo, where many of the large office blocks were still standing (spared, so it was said, by the Americans with an eye to their use during the occupation). Similar waste lands were to be seen at Osaka, Kobe, Nagoya, Shizuoka, Hamamatsu. More than 60 Japanese cities had at least 40 per cent of their built-up area destroyed.

constant traffic, which increased enormously with the coming of peace, of humanity from city to countryside and back to the city again. In order to stay alive many townsfolk bartered their possessions for such surplus food—rice and vegetables—as the farmers could provide. This activity was illegal, since an official rationing scheme was in operation throughout the land. But the old, the very young, and the weak in health could, and did, starve to death if the meagre official ration of food was not supplemented in some way. To perceive the impact of malnutrition on the population in 1945 one need only look at photographs taken in the course of that year. The shabby, patched clothing hangs on the shrunken body of cabinet minister, clerk, labourer,

△ *Erected by Japanese and Americans working side by side, this sign speaks for itself.*
△▷ *Though the occupation began with strict non-fraternisation orders, MacArthur soon found they were impossible to enforce effectively and so modified them by simply designating certain places "Off Limits". This left plenty of opportunity for boy to meet girl – like these two couples by the moat of the Imperial Palace in Tokyo.*

Industrial plant lay in ruins, or, where it survived, was silent due to lack of raw materials. The ferry-boats between the main islands had been sunk by air attack. Shipping of any kind amounted to little more than a total of a million tons (out of some ten million when the war began). There was practically no fuel–except some coal and charcoal. Malnutrition was general. Such items as soap, tobacco, cooking oil, and common medicines were luxuries. Thousands of the homeless squatted in shanties put together from scraps of timber salvaged from the rubble of the great air raids. Others slept out in the railway stations, either permanently or as part of the long wait for the few overcrowded trains that would take them to the countryside. For there was a

or housewife like a loose sack. (Much worse, of course, was the physique of the prisoners-of-war, who looked like skeletons. Liberated from camps in Japan, they had been given even less food than the Japanese and had had no access to a rural black market.)

Japan reorganised

Upon this scene there descended the materially well equipped, confident, more than adequately nourished army of occupation. Very rapidly the best Japanese housing was commandeered for billets, while U.S. army engineers set to work erecting new barrack areas, P.X. stores, and all manner of other buildings for the use of the occupation. The best of the surviving rolling stock on the railways was set aside for the exclusive and free use of the Americans. The Japanese were directed to supply servants for the American billets, and guards and caretakers for the larger installations; and the cost of their wages, like the upkeep of commandeered buildings and rolling stock, was debited to the Japanese authorities.

The Americans imposed their own logical, gridiron pattern of streets and avenues on the haphazard design of Japanese cities. Among the hotchpotch of telegraph poles and advertisement hoardings at big intersections notices began to proliferate in English, proclaiming "Avenue D" or "10th Street". A more striking

all these were endured, accepted indeed, as the inevitable price of surrender. The vital and redeeming feature of the whole situation was that on the whole the behaviour of the occupying forces was not inhumane. It was quickly discovered that the Americans were not addicted to looting, rape, and murder. To this general rule there were but rare exceptions. It is true that S.C.A.P. enforced a strict censorship on press reports reflecting adversely on the occupation. But in a society much given to rumour and gossip, tales of excesses would have been legion if serious misdemeanours and crimes by the Americans had been other than few and far between. The truth in any case emerged after the occupation came to an end in 1952. With the lifting of all press

example of Anglo-Saxon intrusion upon the native scene was the tall American M.P. in white helmet and white gloves directing traffic (nearly all of it non-Japanese); and, standing next to him, imitating every movement of his arms, the relatively diminutive figure of a Japanese traffic policeman.

Hobnailed boots on golden *tatami* rice-straw flooring; painting and varnishing of plain, chaste, wood surfaces; rich food and alcohol in abundance in the midst of semi-starvation; the heated, half empty, S.C.A.P. passenger coach (for occupation personnel only) pushing through the narrow shabby street, past the rare, over-crowded, battered, and painfully slow charcoal-burning Japanese bus; seduction by cigarette carton and candy packet:

restrictions there was a rash of stories, in newspapers and magazines, about the conduct of American troops in the occupation period. These were intended to be sensational. Nearly all were concerned with the immorality of the Japanese girls who attached themselves to G.I.s. What the Japanese had to bear was severe "culture shock". They were not called upon to endure the arrogance and the cruelties which their own servicemen had all too often inflicted upon the Chinese and other inhabitants of the war-time Co-Prosperity Sphere.

Thus in a matter of weeks the worst fears were set at rest—the worst fears on both sides. The Americans, at first suspicious and very much on their guard, found that the Japanese intended to be

△ ◁ The bombed-out residents of Japan's cities found whatever shelter they could, as in these huge concrete sections for water conduits.
△ At the same time, many of the houses that were left standing had been taken over by the occupation forces and, with fraternisation forbidden, notices to this effect were posted outside.

friendly and co-operative. More than this, the civilian population looked to the Americans to set an example of democratic behaviour which the Japanese could follow. Propaganda had led the Japanese to regard their enemies as little better than wild beasts. Close acquaintance after August 1945 totally removed this misconception. The pendulum swung sharply the other way. During at least the first two years of the occupation, American-Japanese relations, at the personal level, were so cordial as to be a kind of honeymoon.

For this there was of course a sound psychological basis. Faith in the traditional structure of state and society had been profoundly disturbed. Only the Imperial house seemed to remain solid among the ruins; and even this institution was now sharply attacked in many quarters. A people accustomed to receiving guidance and direction from on high now turned to the new power in the land, symbolised by General MacArthur and his energetic staff, determined upon their course of reform.

The reforms fell upon the country like an avalanche. The list of those introduced during the first six months of the occupation is impressive indeed. By the end of November 1945 the Imperial armed forces within Japanese territory were fully demobilised. Before November all Japanese laws restricting civil and religious liberties had been suspended, the secret police disbanded, and nationalist groups and organisations broken up and suppressed. In October there came the release of political prisoners; and Communist leaders emerged from the ordeal of many years in jail. Women were given the vote. War criminal suspects, major and minor figures alike, were arrested. The great *zaibatsu,* or financial combines, notably Mitsui, Mitsubishi, Sumitomo, and Yasuda, were split up into small companies. A thorough survey of Japanese educational institutions was put in hand, prior to a drastic reform, including decentralisation, of the whole educational system: meanwhile the teaching of history, with its stress on the patriotic myths of "the divine country", was suspended in schools throughout the land. Martial sports, such as *kendo* (fencing), were banned. Shinto was abolished as a state religion. The first programme of land reform, which would transform tenant farmers into owner-occupiers, was set in motion. In the New Year, 1946, the Emperor made a celebrated public announcement denying

his special status, his so-called "divinity". And in January, too, was launched the "purge" of those, high and low, who had been engaged in notable ultra-nationalist activities. Those involved were excluded from further participation in public life, or government service, at any level. More important, at the end of January 1946 there was published the tentative draft of a new national constitution, modelled closely on the American pattern. These

△ *Demobilised Japanese troops often had no means of livelihood. So these men, pressed into service to help unload supplies for the American occupying forces, were among the lucky ones.*

and the equality of the sexes were by no means novelties for the people of Japan. Like baseball and rugby, they had been known to, and to some degree practised by, the Japanese for years. Back in the 1920's such ideas had won a measure of official acclaim. An intellectually alive and literate population, that had pushed forward from technological backwardness to advanced industrialisation in the space of 50 years, could not be prevented, even by careful police censorship and control, from acquiring a general knowledge of the trends of thought that moved the world beyond Japan. Unfortunately for the Japanese, the dominant, invincible trend of the 1930's appeared to be totalitarianism in its militarist, fascist guise. World events in 1945 showed that this was a misconception.

For some Japanese the S.C.A.P. programme of reforms did not go far enough. Marxism, long driven underground, reappeared as an élite intellectual creed and one that had an appeal for a minority of the urban working class. The more perceptive among Japan's leading statesmen had foreseen that a continuation of a desperately fought and hopeless war could produce social revolution. As early as February 1945 Prince Konoye had warned the Emperor of this possibility. It was appreciated in some circles of big business and the higher bureaucracy that, provided the monarchy and the existing economic order survived, national surrender, however humiliating, was preferable to revolution.

Revolution?

It was the hope, perhaps the expectation, of the extreme Left that surrender would bring revolution in its train, that there would emerge from chaos and disillusionment a People's Republic of Japan. This possibility, no doubt, would have been much enhanced had the occupation been a joint undertaking between the Americans and the Russians. The latter pressed strongly for an equal share in the demilitarisation and reshaping of Japan. Having taken possession of Sakhalin and the Kuriles, the Russians were poised to land in Hokkaido, Japan's northern main island, which seemed the logical area for the establishment of a Soviet zone of occupation in a Japan divided among the war-time Allies.

were only some of the noteworthy reforms carried out or begun on instructions from S.C.A.P. They amounted to a revolution, albeit a peaceful one; and they achieved changes in Japanese society as far-reaching as those that occurred in the last part of the 19th Century after the Meiji Restoration.

That having been said, it is important to bear in mind that such concepts as democracy, the freedom of the individual,

Proposals of this kind were successfully resisted by General MacArthur, who was later backed by Washington. The Russians were invited, as were the Chinese, to send a contingent of troops to Japan, on condition that they were subordinate to MacArthur's headquarters. Neither the Russians nor the Chinese would stomach this. Thus the occupation remained solely an American affair—and in the last resort a one-man affair—for the British Commonwealth Occupation Force, concentrated in the Inland Sea area, had no rôle in the shaping of MacArthur's policy. This policy was indeed nominally subject to the overall authority of the Far Eastern Commission in Washington, an international body in which the United States played the dominant part. In reality MacArthur, supported by a devoted and doting staff, had things very much his own way. Imperious and self-confident, he was to tolerate no interference from the Allied Council, an advisory body in Tokyo composed of representatives of the United States, British Commonwealth, Soviet Union, and China. As for the Far Eastern Commission, its powers on paper seemed impressive. Yet its influence on major policy decisions was very slight. The Commission had to accept the right of the American Government to issue so-called interim directives to S.C.A.P. Moreover, MacArthur's headquarters remained the only authority charged with the implementation of any decisions reached in Washington.

General MacArthur, then, was complete master in his own realm. The Japanese recognised this fact almost from the start. It was in any case sharply underlined in the autumn of 1945, when the Emperor left his palace to pay a call on MacArthur at his office in the Dai Ichi Life Insurance Building. At the time the Emperor's own future appeared uncertain, for he was more than half willing to abdicate in favour of his eldest son. When he met MacArthur, the Emperor declared that he himself, rather than any of his generals and ministers, should be held responsible for the war. The interview went well; MacArthur was favourably impressed by his guest. A photograph, widely distributed by the press, was taken of the two men standing side by side in the Supreme Commander's office. There was no mistaking the balance of power. There was more than a touch of symbolism in the manner in which the older man, relaxed with hands on hips, towered over

△ *A common enough sight in the aftermath of the war. Carrying the ashes of her father in a box covered with a white cloth, a young girl lands at Kagoshima from Okinawa where he was killed in the fighting. She is bringing his remains to be buried near his parents.*

his visitor. Demonstrated here was the style of a new *Shogun,* in whose hands lay the fate of all Japanese, including Emperor Hirohito himself.

Accordingly the Dai Ichi Building became a kind of popular shrine. Day after day at certain regular hours the new *Shogun* passed through its portals, watched by a respectful and admiring crowd. The spectators were for the most part Japanese of all ages, but among them there would nearly always be a sprinkling of G.I.s with their cameras and black-eyed girl friends. The daily routine scarcely varied in six and a half years. MacArthur undertook no tours of his dominion. He left that to the Emperor, who was encouraged to travel among his subjects—a venture in Western-style democratic practice that failed on the whole to be an unqualified success. The Supreme Commander remained notably aloof; and it is difficult to argue that this was a mistake. Indeed conservative Japanese, older men and women in particular, were impressed by his style. S.C.A.P. Headquarters was, after all, a military organisation, in which professional soldiers had more power than civilians or civilians in uniform. It was an order of precedence with which the Japanese were only too familiar.

The new pacifism

On the other hand, in the early days the "New Deal" was well represented in certain sections of the S.C.A.P. apparatus. New Dealers provided much of the enthusiasm and energy behind the reforms that were intended to turn Japanese politics and society upside down. S.C.A.P., then, displayed a mixed, even ambiguous, image. It was the power house, the exemplar, of the fashionable democratic way of life, to which the new Japan was committed. Everyone realised that it was thanks to S.C.A.P. that the new constitution, promulgated in October 1946, came into being; and it was known that MacArthur warmly approved of Article 9, the famous clause in the constitution that committed Japan to eternal pacifism. Nothing made the Japanese prouder—at a time when national pride was in the doldrums—than the feeling that their country, alone in the world, had forsworn an army and navy and the use of force to back up diplomacy. This made Japan unique. It was, therefore, almost universally welcome. Broadly speaking, "progressive" Japanese in the first year or two of the occupation expected much from S.C.A.P. as the agent of necessary change; and the Americans were admired as teachers filled with a missionary zeal, idealistic, and heavy with goodwill.

Yet these teachers were for the most part in uniform; and the best facilities—office blocks, houses, hotels—were reserved for their exclusive use. They might be democrats; but they took strong, sometimes arbitrary, measures against certain categories among the Japanese, not only war criminals and extremists of the old Right but also sympathisers with Russia or North Korea. As time went by it became evident that S.C.A.P. would not tolerate strikes in certain key areas of employment. As daily life improved, rising above a mere struggle to exist, the privileges enjoyed by the Americans (and their female dependants) began to seem tiresome. As the honeymoon started to fade, the inescapably military character of the occupation became oppressive.

The change in the popular attitude developed slowly, and in some quarters was never complete. It was related to world events—the Berlin blockade, the Chinese revolution—which had their effect on American policy, and therefore on the policy of S.C.A.P. The Korean War, a godsend for the still depressed and demoralised Japanese economy, led to the first tentative measures of Japanese rearmament, instigated by S.C.A.P. This awakened old fears. There was a notable slowing down of pressure by S.C.A.P. for the execution of reform programmes. But a hard line was taken against the extreme Left. The emphasis after 1948 was very much on reconstruction rather than reform. Gratifying as this was to the old guard among politicians, businessmen, and bureaucrats, the Japanese Left came to feel itself betrayed by the Americans; and by the time of the Korean War, MacArthur, with his dark glasses and corncob pipe, was in their eyes a baleful, even sinister, figure.

New horizons

The Korean War, which broke out in the summer of 1950, may be taken to mark the end of the period that might be called "Japan in Defeat". For the Korean War boom created the general economic recovery that was to be the basis of Japan's astonishing industrial and commercial growth in the years ahead. But as early as 1947 MacArthur had let it be known that in his opinion the aims of the occupation had been achieved, that the time had arrived for the conclusion of a

treaty of peace. MacArthur was given to rhetoric; yet there is no reason to doubt his sincerity when he declared that the Japanese had become a peace-loving people and that therefore the occupation had served its purpose.

In the case of most countries, at most periods of history, there have been certain fairly predictable reactions to defeat, loss

△ *A Japanese woman and her son burn incense before an altar in their home for the repose of her elder son, killed in action. His portrait, draped with black ribbons, hangs above the altar.*

of territory, and enemy occupation. However subservient to a foreign conqueror a vanquished people may have seemed there has usually been a movement for an eventual war of revenge, as part of a programme of national recovery. This applied to France after 1870, to Germany after 1919.

Now, almost 30 years after August 1945, we can see that in Japan, such reactions to defeat, in so far as they existed at all, were so rare as to count for very little. For this there were many reasons. First and foremost, there was the deep conviction that what was destroyed in 1945 could not be put together again. The old *Tennosei*–the Imperial

An Okinawa laundry girl:
◁ *communicating with a G.I.,*
using schoolgirl English and a
Japanese phrasebook . . .

system bound up with military might and a sense of an invincible national mission– was often thought of as "a golden chalice"; and in 1945 this was shattered, and the pieces could never be reassembled. This remains the belief of the generation that was adult during the Pacific War.

Secondly, the apocalyptic horror of atomic attack provided a face-saving formula for extracting the nation from the war. Thus the Emperor's broadcast could be seen as a positive step, on behalf of humanity everywhere, towards a new and eternal peace, rather than as a negative act of capitulation; and this was fortified by Article 9, the pacifist clause, of the post-war constitution.

Thirdly, the actual fact of defeat in combat on land and sea could not be disguised. If large forces in China and other areas remained unvanquished, there was no disguising the annihilation in conventional warfare that had taken place in the Pacific islands, Burma, the Philippines, Okinawa, Manchuria, and Sakhalin. Similar destruction had been the fate of the Imperial Navy. This great armada had amounted to some two and a quarter million tons when the blow was struck at Pearl Harbor. By August 1945 less than 200,000 tons remained.

The Japanese do not make the same mistake twice. Therefore, complete defeat, it can be claimed, marked the end for ever of an attempt to expand national power by force of arms. And the stupendous economic growth of the 1960's may be seen as part of a process that began almost a hundred years ago, in the late 1870's: a process of determined modernisation through industrial development which was interrupted, or diverted, tragically by the period of aggressive militarism that reached its apogee in the first half of the 20th Century. Interpreted in this light, the obsession with military glory and the expansion of the empire can be regarded as a temporary, although appalling, aberration.

▽ . . . *carrying the washing home . . .*
△ . . . *and pressing the clothes with old-fashioned flat irons. Despite their rather primitive conditions, the family are well off by standards of the time.*

CHAPTER 181

Britain and America in victory

by John Major

VICTORY
OVER GERMANY
1945

GIVE THANKS
BY
SAVING

As World War II reached its climax in 1945, Britain and the United States stood closer together than at any moment since American independence. Their destinies had been interlocked since the fall of France in 1940, when it became clear that Nazi Germany could only be defeated by their combined efforts, and their military collaboration was to go far beyond their association in World War I. It was reinforced still further by the fact that, from their point of view, World War II—even more than World War I—had been fought "to make the world safe for democracy". As the world's two biggest democracies they had affirmed they would set an example of democracy in action, and take on the responsibility of protecting and promoting democracy in the post-war world. The questions which still had to be decided, however, were whether the British and the Americans were willing to make good their war-time pledges in conditions of peace, and whether the circumstances of the peace-time world would allow them to do so. This article examines their reactions in the immediate aftermath of victory.

Let us take first the British political scene. Here the dominant event was the result of the July general election, which swept a Labour Government into power with an overwhelming majority over all its opponents. Before the election the state of the parties had been: Conservatives 361; Labour 166; Liberals 18; Others 69. Afterwards it read: Labour 393; Conservatives 189; Liberals 12; Others 46. In terms of British political history this was the greatest upset since the Liberal landslide of 1906. Seventy-nine of the new Labour constituencies had never returned a Labour M.P. before, and no less than 13 Conservative ministers of cabinet rank went down to defeat.

The basic reason for this dramatic—and largely unexpected—shock was that the Labour Party had succeeded in identifying itself with the demands for a "brave new world" which had gathered force during the war. At the election which followed World War I in 1918, the public had opted for a return to what were supposed to be the "good old days" of pre-1914, and the war-time coalition was given a massive endorsement. In 1945 the situation was utterly different. For too many people "pre-war" meant the grim decade of the 1930's, marked by appeasement of dictatorships abroad and economic depression at home, and it had

Wild scenes greeted the news of victory in Britain's capital.
◁◁ Trafalgar Square on V.E. Day.
△ A beer lorry carrying a load of soldiers—as well as beer—down Piccadilly.
◁ Cementing Anglo-American relations in Piccadilly on V.J. night.
▽ Celebrating crowds throng London's streets on V.J. Day.

been a decade dominated by the Conservative Party. So the Conservatives were damned by the heritage of the recent past. Not even Winston Churchill could save them, even though he had been out of office in the 1930's and even though he had gone on to save his country in 1940 and lead it to victory five years later. The fact that the rebuff was to his party and not to him personally did nothing to salve his bitterness.

The Labour Party, by contrast, under the leadership of Clement Attlee, had convinced the country that it should take Britain into the post-war era, and the conviction was strengthened by the rôle Labour had played in Churchill's coalition, in which Attlee had been deputy premier. In its manifesto, *Let Us Face The Future,* it had promised large-scale economic and social reforms which would build on the experience of the war. The war-time planning of the economy would be continued, underpinned by the nationalisation of key industries such as coal, steel, and inland transport. In the social field, a free national health service and national insurance scheme would come into being to implement the recommendations of the Beveridge Report of 1942. The Conservatives, too, broadly supported Beveridge's proposals and one of their leading figures, R. A. Butler, had sponsored an important new Education Act in 1944. Their acceptance of the need for far-reaching change, however, was lukewarm as compared with Labour's, and so they were rejected. So too were the Liberals, who had adopted a moderate stance between the Big Two and who were now almost extinguished as a political force.

Yet did Labour's tidal wave signal a revolution? Many Conservatives feared it did when they heard that the victors had sung *The Red Flag* at the first meeting of the new House of Commons, but they were wrong. Neither in terms of personalities nor policies was the Labour Government extremist. Attlee himself was a neutral figure who did not deserve the Churchillian gibe that he was "a modest little man with plenty to be modest about", but he was no towering apostle of socialism, and the balance of forces within his cabinet reflected the Party's overall moderation. True, it included two men – Sir Stafford Cripps and Aneurin Bevan – who to date had stood on the far left of the Labour movement, but Attlee's deputy, Herbert Morrison, was a machine politician who had made his reputation as leader of the London County Council,

◄ *H.M. The Queen (now Queen Elizabeth the Queen Mother) meets repatriated prisoners-of-war. Over 1,100 British and Commonwealth servicemen attended the garden party in the grounds of Buckingham Palace.*
▽ *The new Labour Government, elected by the British people in July 1945. Seated, left to right: Lord Addison, Lord Jowitt, Sir Stafford Cripps, Arthur Greenwood, Ernest Bevin, Clement Attlee (the Prime Minister), Herbert Morrison, Hugh Dalton, A.V. Alexander, Chuter Ede, and Miss E. Wilkinson; standing: Aneurin Bevan, G. Isaacs, Lord Stansgate, G.H. Hall, Lord Pethick-Lawrence, J.J. Lawson, J. Westwood, Emmanuel Shinwell, and Tom Williams.*

and the Foreign Secretary, Ernest Bevin, was a trade union boss equally distrustful of revolutionary socialism. As for the party programme, it is worth noting that it sanctioned nothing that had not a wartime precedent and that it left enormous sectors of private activity untouched, including education, health, insurance, and land ownership.

Cautious start

The moderation of the government again showed itself in the slow tempo of its action. There was to be no rush to pass controversial legislation in the first heady flush of victory. Far from cultivating an atmosphere of emergency and keeping the public at the high pitch of excitement reached during the election campaign, Attlee's preference was for measured advance on an orderly basis. So Parliament went into recess at the end of August and by the end of 1945 the only major item of the programme enacted was the nationalisation of the Bank of England.

Labour's cautious début was also dictated by necessity, however, for less than a week after the Japanese surrender it was suddenly made clear that the country might well not have the resources to put through the promised reforms. On August 21 President Truman notified Attlee that America was terminating the Lend-Lease aid which had sustained the British war effort since March 1941. All told, the Americans had disbursed just over $27,000 million to Britain, and the cancellation of the aid immediately put the economy in a desperate position. As the government's chief financial adviser, Lord Keynes, put it, Britain faced "without exaggeration, and without implying that we should not recover from it, a financial Dunkirk".

The disastrous impact of the cutting-off of Lend-Lease can only be appreciated against the background of the losses Britain had suffered as a result of the war. The loss in manpower was the least serious in economic terms – 357,000 dead, or less than one per cent of the population (as opposed to the 11 per cent lost by Germany). Much more damaging economically were the blows that had been delivered to Britain's vital international trade and finance. The merchant fleet was 30 per cent under its 1939 strength after the submarine war, and

exports were running at only 40 per cent of the 1938 level. In the financial sphere, £1,118 million of foreign investments had been sold off, foreign debts had risen by £2,879 million, and gold and dollar reserves had dropped by £152 million. In 1946 a balance of payments deficit of some £750 million was forecast, and given the shattered state of the world economy on which Britain depended, only the United States could save the situation until Britain recovered its balance. If it did not extend more aid, British recovery would be doomed and so too would the Labour programme.

In September, therefore, a British delegation led by Keynes went to Washington to beg for American help. At first they asked for an outright grant of $6,000 million to tide them over the next few years, justifying themselves by citing Britain's war effort. The Americans, however, were interested in future prospects, not past performance, and they drove a hard bargain. A loan of $3,750 million was agreed on, repayable at two per cent interest by the year 2001. These were not unfavourable terms, and especially generous was the wiping out of all but $650 million of the outstanding Lend-Lease debt of $21,000 million. But there were also severe conditions attached to the loan, particularly that British Empire preferences should be reduced and that by July 1947 sterling should be fully convertible into dollars in the world monetary market. These were crippling obligations for the British to accept, but they had no choice and by December 17, only ten days after Attlee's announcement of the settlement, it had been endorsed in both the Commons and the Lords.

Ratification by the U.S. Congress came more reluctantly. The deeply conservative majority of the House of Representatives in particular had strong reservations about lending vast sums of money to a government which they believed was well on the way to communism, and the agreement was not sanctioned until the following July. From this point on the British economy was to be tied to American policy to such an extent as to be ultimately dependent on decisions made in Washington. This was an unpalatable fact for governments in London to swallow, but there was no alternative in sight, for the short-term future at least.

Roosevelt's death a turning point

The situation in the United States during this same period presented a very different picture. There, the political event which controlled all others was the sudden death on April 12, 1945 of President Roosevelt and the swearing-in of his Vice-President, Harry S Truman, as his successor. Truman was very much an unknown quantity. A Senator from Missouri, he had been nominated for Vice-President only in 1944, and he had no experience of executive office. He had

◁ ◁ *Winston Churchill addresses a crowd of about 8,000 in High Wycombe at the start of his election campaign tour. Despite his own immense popularity and prestige, Churchill failed to convince voters that his was the party to lead the country in the coming peace.*
◁ ◁ ▽ *Clement Attlee, leader of the Labour Party, chats to workmen in his own constituency of Limehouse.*
△ ◁ *The fiery Aneurin Bevan was given the Ministry of Health.*
△ *Attlee and other successful candidates from London's East End – Wallie Edwards* (at left), *M.P. for Whitechapel, and Phil Piratin* (behind Attlee), *the new Communist M.P. for Mile End.*

had hit America in 1929. For another he asked for equal job opportunities for Negroes. A little later he sent Congress proposals for a nationwide programme of health insurance and medical care. These and other measures added up to what Truman called the "Fair Deal" and as the new President saw it, they would give substance to the "economic bill of rights" which Roosevelt had called for in his State of the Union message in 1944.

So Truman had made his position clear and he had inherited a comfortable Democratic majority in both houses of Congress: 242 to 190 Republicans in the House of Representatives and 56 to 38 Republicans in the Senate. The temper of the Congress, though, was intensely conservative and the "Fair Deal" suffered in consequence. The unemployment bill was drastically watered down and its provision for mandatory government spending to counteract a depression was cut out. The powers of the administration

Tying up the loose ends of war.
△ *R.A.F. men from the West Indies disembark at Southampton. Their next stop will be the demobilisation depot. Many men, however, chose to be "demobbed" overseas.*
▷ *A sight for the curious—the surrendered German U-776 arriving at Westminster Pier in May 1945. It was on view to the public for two weeks.*
△▷ *and* △▷▷ *The millionth serviceman to pass through the R.A.O.C.'s Civilian Clothing Depot at Inkerman Barracks, Woking. First, Corporal David Moore is measured for his jacket, then he is shown leaving the depot in his full civilian outfit, carrying his military policeman's uniform in a box.*

not been made privy to any of the innermost secrets of policy, and he was stepping into the shoes of a political giant who had been President for longer than any other in American history. Small wonder that many people–perhaps even Truman himself–doubted his capacity for the job.

Whatever his talents, however, Truman was to be President for the best part of four years at least, and it was important to know where he stood on the great issues of domestic and foreign policy. In the domestic field he had yet to make clear his relation to the reformist measures of the New Deal which Roosevelt had pushed through in the 1930's. Many members of the Democratic Party in Congress–especially from the South on which Truman's state bordered–had revolted against the New Deal and formed a conservative alliance with right-wing Republicans. Would Truman give way to them or would he take up the plans which Roosevelt was believed to have been developing for an extension of the New Deal once the war was over?

It was not until the end of the war that Truman was able to reveal his hand. On September 6 he outlined a programme to Congress which placed him squarely in the New Deal camp. For one thing, he proposed that the government should accept an ultimate responsibility to guarantee full employment if private enterprise ran into another depression comparable with the catastrophe which

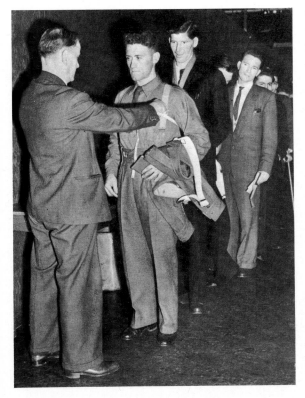

were restricted to reporting annually to Congress on the state of the economy through a three-man Council of Economic Advisers. This was undoubtedly a step forward, but much less than Truman had hoped for. As for the proposals for non-discrimination in employment and medical care, these were to be blocked for some twenty years and were not carried until the presidency of Lyndon Johnson.

The obstructionism in Congress reflected the mood of the country as a whole, however. In Britain, as we have seen, the end of the war was welcomed as the moment to bring in a whole series of reforms. In the United States the reaction was quite different. Once again, as in 1918, there was an overwhelming wish to return to what President Harding had described as "normalcy" and if 1946 had been a presidential election year, there is little doubt that a Republican would have been elected, as Harding was elected in the aftermath of World War I. The

yearning to get back to "normal" was, moreover, reinforced by the fact that—unlike Britain—America had recently undergone a considerable amount of reform in the shape of the New Deal and there was no sense of the need to make up for lost time. Thanks to the various securities provided by the New Deal, indeed, the American people could now afford to indulge in the luxury of reaching out beyond it and demanding a full-blooded return to the affluence they had last enjoyed in 1929.

What is more, the economy was now in a position to gratify them, since the United States was far and away the richest country in the world. Gross national product per head of population in 1946, for instance, stood at just under $1,500 (as compared with $720 in Britain) and in terms of 1929 prices this represented an increase of 50 per cent over the peak attained in the year before the Great Crash. Clearly if America could get through the economic transition from war to peace without serious mishap, it was poised for the greatest boom in its history and one much more solidly based than the frenzied expansion of the 1920's.

The great danger inherent in the situation was, of course, inflation. During the four years of war, most Americans had had high incomes but very little to spend them on. Now they were wild for consumer goods—clothes, cars, furniture, any kind of luxury—and their prices rocketed

△ *For the first time in more than three years, the lights go up on Broadway, the heart of New York's theatreland.*

million. All major industries were affected: coal, oil, steel, electricity, automobiles, the railways.

In all these industries workers were determined not to let their standard of living be undermined by post-war inflation, and to make up for wages lost in the cutback of overtime which accompanied the switch-over from war-time production. At the same time, many feared for their jobs as huge numbers of ex-servicemen flooded back from abroad— no less than nine million were to be demobilised between June 1945 and June 1946.

After the failure of a government-sponsored conference between leaders of labour and management in November 1945, Truman sent a bill to Congress which gave the government authority to declare a strike illegal for a "cooling-off" period of 30 days pending an investigation of its causes. This, however, was not tough enough for the House of Representatives which put forward a rival measure so strongly anti-union that Truman vetoed it. His veto was upheld, but he himself had by then broken a railway strike by threatening, among other things, to call up into the armed forces everyone "on strike against their government". After this the strike movement subsided, but the long-term settlement of industrial conflict in America was still far out of sight.

Strong contrast

The contrast between Britain and America on the domestic side was vivid: the one on the threshold of radical political innovations but with an economy half-crippled by the war; the other rich as never before and with its own burst of reform apparently over. The differences on the international level were equally striking: the United States was now the most powerful nation in the world; Britain, though she retained pretensions to supreme international status, had been reduced to the second rank. During the war the two countries had forged an ironclad partnership, but could it survive in the very different environment of the post-war world?

American power was enormous. The United States had not been bombed or invaded, and their 405,000 dead represented a mere 0.3 per cent of the

accordingly. Truman and his administration were anxious to curb the increases by keeping the price controls introduced during the war which had kept the overall rise to 30 per cent above the level reached in December 1941. Congress, on the other hand, was determined to scrap controls, urged on by lobbies of producers and consumers. The tussle between the two sides ended in June 1946 with a decisive Congressional victory. The immediate result was a rise in the wholesale price index of no less than 25 per cent during the first 16 days of July. This was in direct contrast with Britain, where the public still acquiesced in the many controls retained by Labour and where rationing of most commodities was still strictly enforced. In America the only item rationed at the end of 1945 was sugar.

Finally, Truman had to contend with another symptom of the economic turbulence of the reconversion from war to peace–an unprecedented wave of strikes. During the war the unions had taken a voluntary pledge not to strike, and the government had been given powers to control wages and to act against strikes if they did take place. As a result, only 26 million man-days were lost in the three years 1942-44. In 1945, however, as the war came to a close and wage controls were slackened, the total shot up to 38 million, and in 1946 to a staggering 116

population—as compared with at least 7.6 per cent for the Soviet Union. It had developed a war economy of astonishing potential, manufacturing one ship a day and one aircraft every five minutes, and in June 1945 it had no less than 12 million men and women in uniform, as compared with the five million mobilised by Britain. Its forces were stationed throughout Central Europe, in Germany, Austria, Italy, and Czechoslovakia, while in the Far East they had exclusive control over Japan and the Japanese Pacific islands, as well as troops in China and Korea. Above all, it possessed a monopoly of the atomic bomb which had obliterated the Japanese cities of Hiroshima and Nagasaki in a matter of seconds.

Britain, on the other hand, was a power in decline. The weakness of her post-war economy has been described, and her dependence on American financial aid. In these reduced circumstances it was to prove impossible to maintain her old international position and in particular to hold on to the most obvious symbol of world status, the British Empire. At the close of the war it stood intact, with nearly a quarter of the entire world population united under the British flag, but its future was more limited than anyone could have guessed, and the Victory Parade in London in June 1946 was to be the last occasion on which its forces marched together. Indeed, the British Empire was facing a rapid dissolution under the impact of colonial nationalism, and by the end of the war the balance had already begun to tilt decisively in the nationalists' favour.

It was India which spearheaded the nationalist movement, appropriately enough in view of her huge population of over 400 million and her crucial strategic position at the pivot of the eastern hemisphere. India, in fact, was the linchpin of the whole imperial system, and her loss was to deprive the Empire of its *raison d'être*. Even so, Britain could not withstand the forces of Indian nationalism and within a year after the war a British withdrawal was looming.

The strain on Britain had begun to tell during the war. Under the threat of a Japanese invasion in 1942 independence had been promised once the war was over, but the Hindu majority, organised in the Indian National Congress, had demanded it immediately while the Moslem League, representing the large Moslem minority, had insisted on having its own separate state of Pakistan. Both demands had been successfully resisted, but the writing was on the wall from that moment on.

The accession of the Labour Government at once sent hopes of independence rising. Labour leaders had long been sympathetic to Indian feeling (in contrast

▷ *General of the Army Dwight D. Eisenhower addresses a joint session of Congress on his triumphal return to the United States in June 1945. Earlier, he had been given a hero's welcome by thousands of people as he drove through the streets of Washington in a jeep.*

On January 26, 1946, the Argentina *sailed from Southampton carrying the first contingent of G.I. war brides to the United States.*
△ *A cheerful farewell to family, friends, and the camera.*
△▷ *Arriving in New York on February 9, the G.I. brides were greeted not only by their husbands but by a band supplied by the Army as well.*
△▷▷ *An enthusiastic welcome from U.S. Marine Francis M. Connolly, for his wife, the former Toni Lupino, a passenger on the* Argentina.

with Churchill) and though the King's speech of August 15 spoke only of "the early realisation of full self-government", no one could fail to be aware of how strongly the tide of nationalism was now running. Bitterness against Britain was intense. In November there were massive protests when members of the pro-Japanese Indian National Army were court-martialled, and in February 1946 the Royal Indian Navy mutinied in Bombay. It was highly reminiscent of the upsurge of nationalism after World War I, but Britain was not able to recover her balance as she had done in the 1920's.

It was against this background that elections were held as the preliminary to drawing up a new Indian constitution. All they did, however, was to emphasise the deep split between Congress and the League, and it was beyond the British to get them to co-operate. In August 1946, weeks after a three-man Cabinet mission had drawn up a plan for a united India, communal riots in Calcutta resulted in the deaths of at least 5,000 people. Britain would not only have to "Quit India" as Congress had demanded. She would have to obey the League's summons to "Divide and Quit" and partition the sub-continent which she had forged into a single state.

The coming disengagement from India inevitably had repercussions elsewhere. Second only in importance to India was Egypt, through which ran the vital imperial communications link of the Suez

Canal, to seize which the British had occupied the country in 1882. Although the occupation was over, Egypt was under effective British military control, exercised by a 1936 treaty. During the war the Egyptians had bitterly resented being used as a Middle East strongpoint, and there can be little doubt that if Rommel's *Afrika Korps* had broken through to Cairo in 1942 they would have been welcomed with open arms. In December 1945, therefore, the Egyptian Government asked for a revision of the treaty which would entail the complete withdrawal of British troops, and the move was accompanied by large-scale anti-British riots. Attlee's surprising reply, given on May 7, 1946, was that Britain was ready to negotiate a complete military withdrawal, and talks began soon afterwards. They were to break down, however, over the Egyptian claim to the adjoining territory of the Sudan, which the British denied. So they were left in their Egyptian base but surrounded by a hostile and growing nationalist movement.

The problem of Palestine

In Egypt Britain was able to hold her own; in neighbouring Palestine her position was much more precarious. In 1917 the British Government had promised a "national home" in Palestine for Zionist

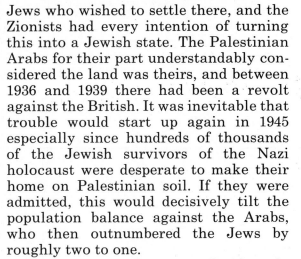

Jews who wished to settle there, and the Zionists had every intention of turning this into a Jewish state. The Palestinian Arabs for their part understandably considered the land was theirs, and between 1936 and 1939 there had been a revolt against the British. It was inevitable that trouble would start up again in 1945 especially since hundreds of thousands of the Jewish survivors of the Nazi holocaust were desperate to make their home on Palestinian soil. If they were admitted, this would decisively tilt the population balance against the Arabs, who then outnumbered the Jews by roughly two to one.

The British reaction was significantly influenced by the pro-Zionism of the American Government and it was in response to pressure from Washington that an Anglo-American commission of inquiry examined the problem early in 1946. Its advice was to admit 100,000 Jews, and this Britain accepted in July, in spite of the recent destruction of British military headquarters in Jerusalem by Jewish terrorists. But the entry of the 100,000 depended on agreement to a plan which would have left Palestine in British hands, and it was clear that neither Arabs nor Jews would submit to that. It was equally clear that the British could not hold out in Palestine much longer.

Given her relative poverty and given the fact that she was now on the defensive in the Empire, Britain had to consider her foreign policy options carefully. Several appeared to lie open. One was a continuation of the war-time "special relationship" with America. Another was the development of a close association with the Soviet Union, an idea attractive to the left wing of the Labour Party and likewise grounded in the comradeship of 1941-45. Alternatively, some Labour members argued, Britain should develop a "Third Force" of countries standing apart from either Russia or America, and consisting of the most progressive states of the British Commonwealth and Europe. Finally, Britain could try to stand alone, drawing on the still considerable resources of the Empire, aloof from Europe and America alike.

America too had not yet fixed her course in the post-war world. After World War I the Senate had repudiated the commitments taken up by President Wilson, and though Roosevelt had affirmed there would be no return to isolation this time, the doubts about Washington's intentions persisted. Perhaps the most solid guarantee of United States policy was their sponsorship of the United Nations, set up to replace the defunct League of Nations which the Senate had refused to join in 1920. Without the strong initiatives which America put behind its development, it is doubtful whether the U.N. would have come into existence. The Charter, signed in San Francisco in

June 1945, bore the imprint of the American vision of a liberal post-war world, and vast sums of money were pledged to ensure that it should work: $2,700 million to the U.N. Relief and Rehabilitation Administration, $2,750 million to the International Monetary Fund, and $3,175 million to the International Bank for Reconstruction and Development. On the other hand, Roosevelt had not anticipated that American forces would stay in Europe for more than two years after the war, and the rate of demobilisation in the armed forces—which were cut from 12 million in June 1945 to only three million a year later—did not suggest that America wished to play a permanent rôle as guardian of world security.

What was also unresolved as yet was the broad attitude which the United States was to adopt towards two of the main political forces of the post-war era, communism and anti-colonialism. The question was even more intriguing since America's two war-time allies, Britain and the Soviet Union, were identified with these forces, directly and indirectly. Russia was the world's foremost communist state and Britain was the world's largest imperial power against which the anti-colonial movement was principally directed. So America's reaction towards these phenomena would effectively determine her policies towards Moscow and London, and ultimately compel the American government to choose between them.

In the perspective of the Cold War there would seem to have been no choice, but at the time the situation was not so clear-cut. Although the United States had a strong anti-communist tradition and although they were themselves completely identified with the capitalism which communism sought to destroy, during the war a certain affinity had developed between Stalin and Roosevelt, based on a mutual recognition of each other's power. Indeed, in 1945 it was apparent that in spite of Russia's devastation, this was the only state in the world which could compare with America as a "super-power". Between them they straddled the world, and several members of the Truman administration believed that international affairs would best be governed by their continued co-operation.

At the same time, Americans had long been hostile to British imperialism. They owed their very independence to a successful struggle against it, and during the war there had been forceful criticism

of British policy in India and elsewhere. Anti-colonial pressure had been kept up during the drafting of the U.N. Charter (with enthusiastic Russian support), and the Americans had managed to have written into it a declaration on colonies aimed at exerting some pressure on colonialist member-states to move their

The transition from wartime to a peace-time economy was not always achieved smoothly.
△ *A one-man protest by a disabled ex-Marine unable to resume his pre-war occupation.*
▽ *Students demonstrate in support of strikers at Warner Brother's studio, Hollywood.*

△ Post-election tension in Tennessee, where the G.I. Independent Party ousted the Democrats and feared an attempt to regain control by force.
▽ Trouble at a Pratt & Whitney plant as non-union workers try to break the picket line. The strike lasted over eight weeks.

territories towards independence. Therefore as Britain and other colonial powers attempted to come to grips with their problems after 1945 they did so without American sympathy or support. In taking this attitude, Americans seriously overestimated British strength. As we have seen, the Empire was no longer a secure

basis of international power, but for some time to come American policies went on being influenced by the views of the past.

This came out forcefully in the wrangle over atomic energy which soured relations in the early part of 1946. During the war British scientists had collaborated with the Americans in developing the bombs which annihilated Hiroshima and Nagasaki, and Churchill had secured a pledge from Roosevelt that the teamwork would go on after the war. In November 1945 Attlee believed he had been given a similar promise by Truman which provided for "full and effective co-operation in the field of atomic energy" between America, Britain, and Canada. In April 1946, however, when Attlee asked for detailed information on atomic energy plants, Truman refused. Part of the reason was that the Americans did not trust British security (with good reason), but the information had also been denied to make it that much more difficult for Britain to develop as an atomic power in her own right.

No threat from Britain

What began to change American suspicions of Britain as a rival force in world affairs was the dawning realisation that Britain could not in fact present a real threat to American interests. Russia, on the other hand, could and did challenge the United States' global position, and there was a growing body of opinion within the Truman administration which was not only prepared to take this challenge up, but even to support the imperialist interests of Britain in the broader concern to counter Soviet policies.

The change took time to make itself felt in American thinking. In March 1946, for example, when Churchill made his famous "Iron Curtain" speech, claiming that Russia was a dangerous expansionist power, Washington took care not to associate itself with the view, although Truman sat next to Churchill on the platform. Six months later, however, the leading American advocate of Soviet-American collaboration, Henry Wallace, was dismissed by Truman for making a speech in which he called for a recognition of the Soviet sphere of influence in Eastern Europe and named Britain as the greatest impediment to progress through-

3051

△ Porters at New York's Grand Central Station idle their time away during the massive railroad strike which gripped the United States in May 1946. Only hospital, milk, and troop trains were kept running during the dispute.

By the terms of a common agreement, although Germany was divided into four occupation zones, there was an obligation to treat it as a single economic unit. Therefore the predominantly industrial British and American zones were required to send the Russians industrial products and equipment as reparations, while the primarily agricultural Soviet zone was obliged to send in foodstuffs in return. The Russians, however, were not keeping their end of the bargain, and the British and American occupation commands were having to import food on a large scale. During 1946 this was to place an extra burden of no less than £80 million on the already overstrained British economy, and so Britain welcomed the American proposal, made in July, to fuse its zone with any other. The load was spread and Anglo-American co-operation began to take firm shape.

out the world. By the end of the year the shift in American policy was practically complete.

To some degree it was a reflection of the revival of American conservatism immediately after the war, a perhaps inevitable reaction against the long reign of Roosevelt and the New Deal. Anti-communism was a natural ingredient of this new mood and it was to prove a vote-winner right through the first post-war decade. But Soviet policies also played their part, even if only in reaffirming a basic conviction that the U.S.S.R. was America's obvious enemy. Already in 1945, for instance, the Russians had begun to encroach on the Middle East by attempting to extend their influence in Turkey and Iran, and they were suspected (wrongly) of giving military aid to the communist partisan forces in the Greek civil war. In the case of Turkey and Iran, the American reaction was a prompt and unequivocal rejection of the Soviet claims. In the case of Greece, Washington could still rely on Britain, which had been holding the ring since the end of 1944, but in view of British economic weakness it was doubtful how long this could go on. So America was gradually assuming a commitment to resist Russian penetration which Britain had held since the end of the 18th Century.

In Germany, too, Soviet policies helped to make it impossible for the Americans to withdraw from Europe, and here again Soviet actions pushed Britain and the United States together.

A time of hope

For both Britain and the United States, the first 12 months or so after the war were a time of hope. Hope in Britain that a more just society could–this time–emerge from the bleakness of total war. Hope in America that the ghost of depression had finally been laid and that happy days really were here again, and to stay. Nothing could have been more different than these two approaches to the future, the high-minded austerity of social democracy and the rush towards affluence in its liberal counterpart, and the divergences did not augur well for Anglo-American co-operation; nor did the several clashes of national interest and opinion–over Zionism, atomic weapons, colonialism, the position of sterling. And yet co-operation was reviving in spite of the differences because of a sense of common danger emanating from Stalinist Russia. This feeling may have been misplaced, but it would have been asking too much of any government to ignore it. To base policy on distrust of the Soviet Union was, of course, to accept that three-power unity had not survived the war. But it also meant that two of those powers were united, and that the expectations of a new world need not be abandoned. Had Britain and America gone their separate ways, as they did a quarter of a century before, then they almost certainly would have been.

CHAPTER 182
The War Trials

The decision to bring Axis "war criminals" to justice was taken by the Allies quite early in World War II. With the Nazi conquest of western European countries in 1940, and of Yugoslavia and Greece in 1941, came reports of millions of men and women being forced to work in German factories and mines, and of occupation régimes relying on taking and executing hostages to maintain order. Later came the story of the Nazis' "final solution to the Jewish problem", or the mass extermination of Jews. Churchill and Roosevelt made simultaneous statements on October 25, 1941, warning that retribution would certainly follow in the wake of such war crimes. The governments-in-exile in London joined in this protest, and on January 13, 1942, representatives of these nine governments–Belgium, Czechoslovakia, the Free French National Committee, Greece, Luxembourg, the Netherlands, Norway, Poland, and Yugoslavia–adopted the Declaration of St. James, in which the signatories declared that among their principal war aims was the punishment, through organised channels, firstly of those responsible for instituting in occupied countries a régime characterised by imprisonment, mass expulsion, execution

of hostages, and massacres; and secondly of those guilty of perpetrating or participating in such atrocities. On January 9, 1942, the Chinese Government accepted the principles of the declaration, and in October of that year, the U.S.S.R. also subscribed.

On October 7, 1942, with the support of the U.S., Great Britain, and 15 other Allied governments, the United Nations War Crimes Commission was established in London. Its main function was to gather information regarding war crimes and suspects, and to formulate rules of procedure for the courts where the criminals would be tried. The Commission began regular work in January 1944, and in addition, carried out extensive investigations on the theory of law.

At the Yalta Conference, the Allies stated their intention to bring all war criminals to just and swift punishment, and at Potsdam, they talked of "stern justice".

On August 8, 1945, the four major victorious powers–U.S.A., U.S.S.R., Britain, and France–signed the London Agreement setting up the International Military Tribunal (I.M.T.) in Nuremberg, which was to try the major war criminals of the

△ *Just after his capture, Göring gives a press conference for Western journalists. Despite his resplendent uniform, giving an air of authority, the former Deputy Führer was at this time a virtual wreck–both mentally and physically. To start with, he was a drug addict–"a simpering slob", according to the prison commander. But proper medical treatment and the strict régime of prison life soon brought about a remarkable recovery.*

European Axis.

The trial, which began in November 1945 and lasted almost ten months, was a monumental undertaking by all legal standards. The defendants were the military, political, and economic leaders of the vanquished Nazi Reich, namely Göring, Ribbentrop, Keitel, Kaltenbrunner, Frank, Frick, Rosenberg, Streicher, Sauckel, Jodl, Seyss-Inquart, Hess, Funk, Raeder, Schirach, Speer, Neurath, Dönitz, Schacht, Papen, and Fritzsche. The trial was conducted in four languages simultaneously – English, German, Russian, and French. The tribunal held 403 open sessions, with 33 witnesses appearing for the prosecution, which also submitted 4,000 documents in evidence. Sixty-one witnesses appeared for the defence, in addition to 19 of the defendants. Reported evidence in the trial comprises 24 printed volumes and 17 additional volumes of documents. Eleven of the accused received death sentences.

There were a further 12 international trials held at Nuremberg.

Basic policy for the trial and punishment of Japanese war criminals was the *Proclamation Defining Terms for Japanese Surrender* of July 26, 1945, usually referred to as the Potsdam Declaration. An International Military Tribunal was established at Tokyo, and 28 defendants were tried. The tribunal was composed of members from 11 nations, namely the United Kingdom, the U.S.A., China, the U.S.S.R., France, the Netherlands, Canada, Australia, New Zealand, India, and the Philippines. The tribunal sentenced seven defendants to death by hanging.

As well as these international trials, there were also the orthodox military channels of justice. For example, in Europe, the United States Army judge advocate was responsible for the prosecution of crimes against American troops, and in Nazi concentration camps liberated by American forces. Army military commissions and courts tried some 1,600 German war criminals and sentenced over 250 defendants to death. The same numbers were tried by the British, the French, and by countries which had suffered Nazi occupation. There are no figures available for courts held in Russia or China, and in West Germany the numbers are incomplete as war criminals are still pursued today and brought to trial.

The war crimes trials led to a flood of controversy over what constituted a war

Joachim von Ribbentrop was Minister for Foreign Affairs from 1938 onwards. For two years before that he had been Ambassador in London, where he formed the opinion that Britain would not honour her guarantees to Poland. He was an early, and close, adherent of Hitler's–who, in turn, was impressed by Ribbentrop's social graces. His influence waned throughout the war and by the end this "vain and incompetent" man was thoroughly disgraced. Hanged.

crime and a war criminal, and over whether in fact the trials were legal or not. There was no law in 1939 according to which the dreadful atrocities which took place could be considered crimes. At the Nuremberg trial, the defendants were charged on the following counts: the crime of being party to a common plan or conspiracy to wage wars of aggression, or crimes against peace; war crimes; and crimes against humanity. What precedent was there for such a trial?

The charges were based partly on the ancient code of conduct in war whereby although it is recognised that war consists largely of acts that would be considered criminal in times of peace, for example, killing people and destroying property, it is not acceptable, even in war, to inflict suffering for its own sake, or for revenge.

American example

This principle was given explicit written form for the first time in 1863 in the U.S. War Department's *Instructions for the government of armies of the United States in the field,* which covered crimes against inhabitants of hostile countries, and prisoners-of-war, for example.

Further formalisation of these laws of war and their embodiment in international agreements was called for after the Franco-Prussian War. Consequently, The Hague and Geneva Conventions were made, the most important of these being the 4th Hague Convention of 1907, and the Geneva Prisoners-of-War and Red Cross Conventions of 1929.

The Fourth Hague Convention sets forth requirements and limitations with regard to the conduct of hostilities, treatment of prisoners-of-war, and the exercise of authority over occupied territory of a hostile state. Accordingly, enemy soldiers who surrender must not be killed, but must be taken prisoner; captured cities must not be pillaged, nor undefended places bombarded. Arms calculated to cause unnecessary suffering are forbidden. The convention stated that war is not a free-for-all, and that only members of the armed forces can be protected by the laws of war. An army in occupied territory must respect family rights, people's lives, and also their religious convictions.

The Geneva and Red Cross Conventions gave ruling on the treatment of P.O.W.s,

Rudolf Hess, Deputy Führer 1933-1941, had taken part in the 1923 abortive Munich *Putsch*. Completely loyal, Hess believed he was interpreting Hitler's wishes when he flew to Scotland on a peace mission. But Hitler disowned him and the British treated him as a P.O.W. The question of his sanity has never been settled. Life imprisonment.

◁ *The courtroom at Nuremberg. At the tables are, from left to right, the British, U.S., and Russian prosecution teams.*
▽ *Hess with Colonel John Amen, interrogation chief at Nuremberg.*

Franz von Papen was appointed Reich Chancellor (briefly) in 1932 and was subsequently Vice-Chancellor in Hitler's government for a short time. He was later given a series of unimportant diplomatic posts. Acquitted.

△ *Representatives on the War Crimes Commission. From left: Professor Trainin and General Nikitchenko (U.S.S.R.); Lord Jowitt (U.K.); Mr. Justice Robert Jackson (U.S.A.); and M. Falco (France).*

and on the relief of the sick and wounded.

There were no agreements at this time on naval warfare in general, although the Ninth Hague Convention prohibited the bombardment of undefended ports, and the London Naval Treaty of 1930 outlawed the sinking of merchant ships by submarines unless the passengers and crew were first moved out of harm's way.

These, then, were the laws of war – principles which found written expression in these treaties and agreements, embodiments of an ancient, established code of conduct, which had developed through custom and practice. Indeed, many countries, including the United States, Britain, France, and Germany, absorbed the laws of war into their military laws, and the military organisation of the 18th Century had led to the establishment of military courts to enforce these laws, and to try those who transgressed.

The trial of Sir Peter of Hagenbach in 1474 is a very early example of a war crimes trial. In 1469, Duke Charles of Burgundy forced the Archduke of Austria to pledge to him his possessions on the upper Rhine. Hagenbach was made governor of Breisach on the upper Rhine, where he instituted a régime of terror. His crimes were unique

in their savagery, even in those dangerous times. When the area was recaptured, Hagenbach was tried in Breisach for his crimes by order of the Archduke of Austria. His judges were from Austria and allied cities. Hagenbach pleaded that he acted in conformity with his orders, but he was sentenced to death, and beheaded in the market place. It is important to note here that Hagenbach was accused only of murder, and that he had committed his crimes before the beginning of the war.

The case of Napoleon, banished to St. Helena, is a precedent of international action for the treatment of a defeated enemy.

World War I

After World War I, the Allied "Commission on the responsibility of the authors of the war and on enforcement of penalties" met on January 25, 1919, to recommend the necessary action to be taken against enemy nationals accused of having committed war crimes. This meeting resembled the London Conference of the four major victorious powers in August 1945, as in

Dr. Ernst Kaltenbrunner was chief of the Reich Main Security Office from 1943 onwards, following Heydrich's assassination. This "tough, callous ox" was earlier appointed Austrian Minister of Security. As Himmler's deputy in the R.S.H.A. and head of the *Abwehr* he controlled all the security and terror organisations in the Reich. It was said that even Himmler feared him. He denied all knowledge of mass murders, but the evidence against him was overwhelming. Hanged.

Alfred Rosenberg, Minister for the Occupied Eastern Territories, was the main philosopher of the Nazi Party. His book, *The Myth of the Twentieth Century,* provided Hitler with a pseudo-scientific basis for his Aryan fantasies and anti-Semitic rantings. Head of the Party's Foreign Affairs Office from 1933, Rosenberg was appointed administrator of occupied Russia in 1941. His *Einsatzstab Rosenberg* unit removed art treasures from conquered territories. Hanged.

Baldur von Shirach was Leader of the Hitler Youth from 1931 and Reich Youth Leader from 1933 onwards. In 1940 he was appointed *Gauleiter* and Defence Commissioner of Vienna, a post he held until the end of the war. In his capacity as Youth Leader he was implicated in the forcible moving of thousands of young people from occupied territories into Germany; while in Vienna he was responsible for deporting some 60,000 Jews to eastern Europe. Twenty years' imprisonment.

Albert Speer, Reich Minister for Armaments and War Production, was Hitler's close friend. His brilliant organisational ability meant that, despite air raids, war production actually increased during 1943 and early 1944. But as head of the Todt Organisation he was also held responsible for using slave labour. Twenty years' imprisonment.

▽ *Kaltenbrunner defends himself from the dock.*

Previous page: *The leaders of Nazi Germany in the dock.*
▽ *The cell where Robert Ley, former leader of the German Labour Front, hanged himself before the opening of the trial. He had, remarked Göring, "been drinking himself to death anyway".*
▷ △ *A revitalised Göring in the witness box. He conducted a spirited defence, frequently scoring points off the prosecution.*
▷ ▽ *A chalk and wash sketch by Dame Laura Knight, showing Göring, Hess, Ribbentrop, and Keitel. She made several such sketches during the course of the trial, as preliminaries for a large and comprehensive oil painting.*

Julius Streicher had taken part in the abortive Munich *Putsch*. He called himself the "Jew-baiter Number One", and as such owned and edited *Der Stürmer*, which poured out a steady stream of scurrilous anti-Semitism. He was appointed *Gauleiter* of Franconia in 1925. He was a gross, coarse man with a conspicuously low I.Q., notable for his corruption even by Nazi Party standards. In 1940 he was dismissed for misappropriating confiscated Jewish property. Hanged.

Constantin von Neurath was Foreign Minister from 1932 to 1938 and *Reichsprotektor* of Bohemia and Moravia until 1941. From 1901 he made his career in the foreign service but nevertheless made no objection to serving in Hitler's government. As *Reichsprotektor* he supervised the brutal supression of Czech resistance, but the court accepted that he had tried to restrain the work of the Gestapo. Later Neurath was involved in anti-Hitler plots. Fifteen years' imprisonment.

Hjalmar Horace Greeley Schacht was President of the Reichsbank from 1933 to 1939 and Minister of Economics 1935-37. This American-born financial genius became Hitler's monetary adviser in 1930 but never joined the Nazi party. He resigned both his posts after disagreements withHitler over economic matters and Germany's preparation for war. His anti-war views were well known to his American contacts. Arrested and imprisoned after the July 1944 plot. Acquitted.

Reichsmarschall Hermann Goring, C.-in-C. Luftwaffe and Air Minister, was Hitler's No. 2. in the Nazi hierachy. He joined the Party in 1922 and rose rapidly in the ranks to become one of the "inner circle". His rather coarse bonhomie made him perhaps the most popular of Germany's leaders, but his drive and energy became increasingly dissipated by drug addiction and self-indulgence. At the trial he was revealed as a bullying, shrewd, and intelligent showman. Condemned to death, he committed suicide just before the execution.

Colonel-General Alfred Jodl, was chief of Operations Section, O.K.W. from 1938 onwards. In this post he worked closely with Hitler and the Commander-in-Chief on all German campaigns. His task was to keep Hitler informed of the military situation, but all too often his assessment was faulty. A clever man, Jodl managed to retain his position in the high command throughout the war while many other generals were sacked. At the trial he pleaded "soldier's obedience" to excuse the way he condoned illegal acts by the German armed forces. Hanged.

As in other recently-liberated countries, the new-found patriotism and enthusiasm of the French found an outlet in revenge. People hit back at those whose collaboration had been more than mere acquiescence.

△ The cabinet at Vichy, including Pierre Laval (5), Marshal Pétain (8), and General Weygand (10), all of whom were arrested and accused of collaboration after the war. The unfortunate Weygand (who had already been imprisoned by the Germans) was acquitted, but Laval and Pétain were both sentenced to death. Laval was executed, Pétain—in view of his advanced age and previous service to France—was reprieved.

▷ Laval speaks during his trial for treason.

Wilhelm Keitel was O.K.W. Chief-of-Staff. A man of poor mental and moral calibre, he idolised Hitler, who described him as "a man with the brains of a cinema usher". He had served with the artillery in World War I. He retained his position because Hitler did not care for a more able officer as Chief-of-Staff and partly because of the ability of his own Chief-of-Staff, Jodl. The perfect lackey, he earned the nickname *Lakaitel* or "Little Lackey". Hanged.

Karl Donitz was chief of the German Navy, U-boat strategist, and Hitler's deputy. From experience in World War I he evolved the "Wolf Pack" U-boat tactics for operating against merchant convoys. He succeeded Admiral Raeder as Naval C.-in-C. in January 1943. At the end of the war Hitler nominated him as successor, and though Dönitz attempted to make peace with the West he eventually had to accept the unconditional surrender. Ten years' imprisonment.

Arthur von Seyss-Inquart was Reich Commissioner of the Netherlands. He employed a policy of which he said "We demand everything that is of use to the Reich and suppress everything that may harm the Reich." He expropriated works of art, deported Jews, and waged a savage war against the Resistance during his term of office from 1940 to 1944. He sent 5 million men to work as labourers in the Reich. He was arrested by the Canadians in May 1945. Hanged.

1919 the violations for which the German leaders were considered liable were much the same as those included in the Nuremberg Charter.

The Commission report after World War I stated that all enemy persons who had violated the laws and customs of war and the laws of humanity should be liable to criminal prosecution, regardless of their rank or authority. The report stipulated that, under international law, a person could be tried by his captors for such violations. The Commission recommended setting up a High Tribunal to try the accused, and it is interesting to note that while the majority of the Allied nations endorsed this recommendation, the American delegates objected to the creation of an international criminal court on the grounds that a precedent was lacking.

Many recommendations made by the Commission were incorporated into the articles concerning punishment of war criminals in the Peace Treaty of Versailles, and on February 3, 1920, the Allied powers submitted to the German delegate at the peace conference a list of 896 names of persons to be handed over for trial. The German Government had no intention of turning over the accused and declared that they should stand trial by the Supreme Court of the Reich in Leipzig. The Allies finally consented to this, with the result that very few persons were actually convicted, and of those who were, several escaped from German prisons.

And so ended the most important attempt prior to Nuremberg by several nations to institute judicial proceedings against nationals of a vanquished state for alleged war crimes. However, the Leipzig trials conducted by the German Supreme Court affirmed that violations of the laws of war are punishable offences.

Legal problems

But as there is no international legislature, the laws of war can have no statutory form, and nowhere are the means of enforcement or the penalties for violation specified. The question is, is it satisfactory to say that international law, and in particular the laws of war, have evolved over time, through usage, in very much the same way as English common law developed in pre-Parliamentary times? Are these laws binding on states?

The problem of laws evolving through

LA DOMENICA DEGLI ITALIANI

ITALIA	ESTERO		
Anno . . . . L. 335,-	L. 360,-		
Semestre . . . . . . » 190,-	» 205,-		

Spedizione in abbonamento postale - Gruppo 2

Si pubblica a Milano ogni settimana

Per le inserzioni rivolgersi all'Amministrazione del Corriere d'informazione
Via Solferino N. 28 - Milano

UFFICI DEL GIORNALE:
VIA SOLFERINO N. 28 - MILANO

Per tutti gli articoli e illustrazioni è riservata la proprietà letteraria e artistica, secondo le leggi e i trattati internazionali.

Anno I - N. 22   21 Ottobre 1945   L. 7.- la copia

I criminali del campo di Belsen. Nell'aula del Tribunale alleato a Lüneburg, il capo degli aguzzini, Josef Kramer (contrassegnato col numero 1) la sua amante Irma Greese (numero 9) e una quarantina di altri imputati.

practice was foreseen at the Fourth Hague Convention, whose preamble had this to say on subjects not actually covered by this, or any other, convention: these questions should be resolved by "the principles of the law of nations, as they result from usages among civilized peoples, from the law of humanity, and from the dictates of public conscience". The Nuremberg Tribunal, and the 12 subsequent military trials, all confirmed that it was quite proper for international law to evolve in this way. It is important to note that nations are regarded as bound by the laws of war whether or not they were signatories to the Hague and Geneva Conventions.

Individual status

Following closely on from this question is that of whether or not individuals are subject to international law. This is an important question, for nearly all individuals are nationals of a certain state, regarding obedience to that state's laws as their highest obligation.

The underlying principle at the war crimes trials was that there are some standards of behaviour that transcend the duty of obedience to national laws. War is an obligation to kill for reasons of state, but it does not grant a licence to kill for personal reasons, and it does not coun-

tenance the infliction of suffering for its own sake or revenge. These latter actions would still rank as criminal even in wartime.

The problem of superior orders was not a new one at the war crimes trials following World War II. Almost universally it has been ruled that if the accused was aware that the order called for the commission of a criminal act, then his obedience is punishable as a criminal offence. However, what was criminal and what was not was very hard to determine. A soldier regards his duty as obedience to his military superiors. If he does not obey, he could suffer heavy punishment or even death. To disobey, therefore, calls for a very high degree of moral courage. However, according to international law, he must obey only lawful orders.

Some orders are so atrocious that the subordinate must know that they should not be obeyed. It was the case in Nazi Germany, though, that some of the defendants at Nuremberg obeyed the most horrific orders not fearfully and unwillingly, but often approvingly and with great enthusiasm. Relations between the leader and the led did not preclude individual responsibility if the followers knew Hitler's aim and co-operated in the achievement of that aim. Only top servicemen could be accused of *planning* an aggressive war, but others–Dönitz for example–were tried for *waging* an aggressive war.

Wilhelm Frick was a long-term member of the Nazi Party, and had been in Hitler's first cabinet. In 1939 he was Minister of the Interior, but the police, whom he had nazified and centralised, were under the control of Himmler. In August 1943 he was removed from the central government and made *Protektor* of Bohemia and Moravia. He was convicted of planning aggressive war and of committing crimes against humanity. Hanged.

◄ *The trial at Lüneburg of S.S. Captain Josef Kramer and his associates from Bergen-Belsen.*
△ *The trial of Vidkun Quisling in Norway, August 1945. He was convicted of treason and executed in the same year.*

◁ *The summation of the tribunal and the verdict in the process of being assembled. Each of the Allied nations produced a translation of the tribunal's report. Even the defendants, their counsel, and contemporary opinion in Germany admitted that it had been a fair trial.*

3068

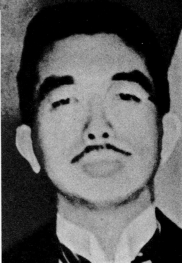

Hirohito, Emperor of Japan, whose full title was "Imperial Son of Heaven of Great Japan". Though the power to wage war, declare peace, and make treaties lay with him, it was exercised according to his ministers' advice. He lacked firmness when dealing with the war-mongering chiefs-of-staff. He remained in the background during the early successes, but later Tojo tried to involve him. The people were reminded of his divine destiny and promised the ultimate victory. In August 1945 he began to urge peace. On the 15th, a day after the surrender, he broadcast to his people for the first time in Imperial history. Although named as a war criminal by China, New Zealand, and Australia, he was granted immunity since the major powers felt that responsibility for the war did not lie with him. He played an important part in the post-war reconstruction of Japan by offering the people an apolitical leadership.

◁◁ *The Emperor Hirohito inspects his troops in the days of Japan's new military ascendency.*
◁△ *Japanese crowds bow before the Emperor's car. Japan was a nation which, though armed and equipped with the products of the 20th Century, still lived in the style of the 12th. For them the Emperor was a divine being descended from the sun. In reality he was a shy introverted man whose chief interest was marine biology. He had written a book on shellfish based on specimens he had collected personally.*

Perhaps it is a different matter in the lower ranks, where unquestioning obedience to orders is a necessity of military life. If a soldier is to give such obedience, perhaps he should be defended from charges of unlawful conduct. Besides, it is the responsibility of the superior officer to see that troops do not commit war crimes. The most notable case of a commander's failure to discharge this responsibility was tried by a United States military commission in Manila. The defendant was General Tomayuki Yamashita, Japanese commander in the Philippines in the closing stages of the war. At this time, the conduct of Japanese troops on the Philippine Islands degenerated, and many prisoners-of-war were massacred along with civilians, and arson and looting were rife. General Yamashita had not ordered this, and perhaps he did not even know about it. He was judged not to have adequate control of his troops and he was sentenced to death by hanging in 1946.

Let us now consider the International Military Tribunal at Nuremberg itself. Britain, the United States, Russia, and France conducted the trial, and the objection has been made that a tribunal need not be considered international and binding on states which were not contracting parties to the treaty or agreement that forms its basis. No German government subscribed to the Charter nor gave its

▷ *Japanese war criminals awaiting trial in Changi Jail on Singapore Island. Some 700 men were detained as suspect war criminals. The picture shows men copying coloured pictures from magazines. Their brushes are made from human hair. Their jailers reported that many detainees were extremely proficient.*

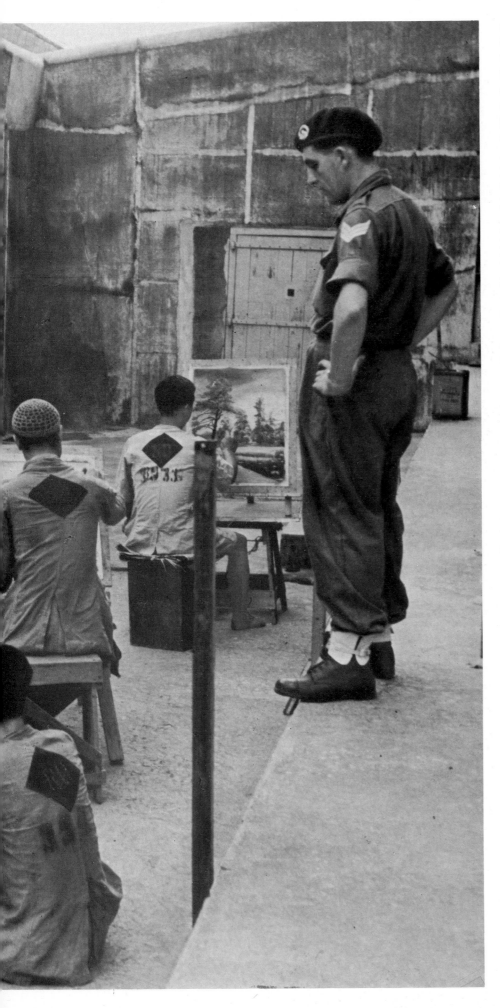

consent to the Tribunal's jurisdiction over German nationals, and on these grounds, the I.M.T. was not legal. It has been contended that the I.M.T. was no more than an inter-Allied occupation tribunal, staffed exclusively with Allied personnel. Some of the judges had actually participated in drafting the I.M.T. Charter. The Allied captors hence created the law, prepared the indictments, produced the evidence, conducted the prosecution, and judged the defendants.

The criticism that the tribunal was composed entirely of nationals of victorious powers is a serious moral one. It is thought that some neutral judges would have made for a fairer judgement, but which state in 1945 was a real neutral, and would such a state have welcomed involvement?

The objection has also been raised that a Soviet judge was placed on the tribunal, when the Soviet Union was just as guilty as Germany in launching aggressive war against Poland. However, it is legally irrelevant whether or not war criminals existed in the Allied camp. It is never open to a murderer to object to his trial on the grounds that there are other untraced murderers at large. It is no defence to say that others have committed the crime for which he is being tried.

The charges

The charges on which the defendants at Nuremberg were tried were waging aggressive war or crimes against peace, war crimes, and crimes against humanity.

On the subject of waging aggressive war, the Allied commission after World War I concluded that the initiation of an aggressive war, while morally reprehensible, was not an act directly contrary to positive law. In the inter-war years, several treaties, including the Kellogg-Briand Pact of 1928, prohibited wars of aggression and condemned war as an instrument of policy. This was accepted by the U.S.A., France, and 42 other nations, but did this pact mean that aggressive war was now unlawful? In 1944, the U.N. War Crimes Commission was divided on this question and could not come to a decision. The fact that the terms "aggression" and "international crime" were not defined did nothing to help clarify the situation. However, the parties to the Nuremberg Charter decided that aggression was a crime, and so rendered ineffective further arguments

△ *Japanese war criminals, among them Hideki Tojo, enter the War Ministry building in Tokyo to be arraigned before the International War Crimes Tribunal.*
▷▷ *Captain George A. Furnese, defence counsel, addresses the court.*

General Sheishiro Itagaki was War Minister from 1938 to 1940. He was an active member of the Army conspiracy which brought Japan into the war. From April 1945 he was commander of Japanese forces in Java, Sumatra, Malaya, Borneo, and the Andaman and Nicobar Islands. Charged with crimes relating to death and maltreatment of prisoners of war and civilian internees. Hanged.

Colonel Kingore Hashimoto, soldier and propagandist. Leader of the *Sakura-kai* or Cherry Society, he aimed to "purify the national life". Though he was an outspoken advocate of aggressive war there was no evidence to link him with the crimes contravening the laws and customs of war. He had become fascinated by dictatorship while in Europe. Life imprisonment.

General Kuniaki Koiso, Prime Minister. The Tribunal argued that during Koiso's office it had become public knowledge that troops were guilty of excesses in all theatres. In October 1944 his foreign minister said that Japanese treatment of Allied P.O.W.'s left "much to be desired". During his last six months of office conditions for prisoners did not improve. For "deliberate disregard of his duty" life imprisonment.

3073

General Sado Araki, Minister of War from 1931 to 1934. An advocate of the Army's policy of domination at home and aggression abroad, he was a general in 1933 and was prominent in the upper councils of the Army. He not only played an active rôle in the campaigns in Manchuria and Jehol, but did much to stimulate the warlike impulses in Japanese youth. He was found guilty of waging an aggressive war against China. Life imprisonment.

Admiral Shigetaro Shimada, Navy Minister from October 1941, and privy to all the government decisions from the attack on Pearl Harbor onwards. The Tribunal held that he was not responsible for the "disgraceful massacres and murders" of prisoners and the crews of torpedoed ships committed by the Navy. He was found guilty of participating in the planning and waging of an aggressive war between October 1941 and August 1944. Before then he had been employed solely on Naval duties. Life imprisonment.

◁ *The accused stand as the judges enter.* Front row, left to right: *Doihara, Hata, Hirota, Minami, Tojo, Oka, Umezu, Araki, Muto, Hoshino.* Back row, left to right: *Koiso, Nagano, Oshima, Matsui, Hiranuma, Togo, Matsuoka, Shigemitsu, Sato, Shimada, Shiratori, Itagaki.* In front are the defence counsel.

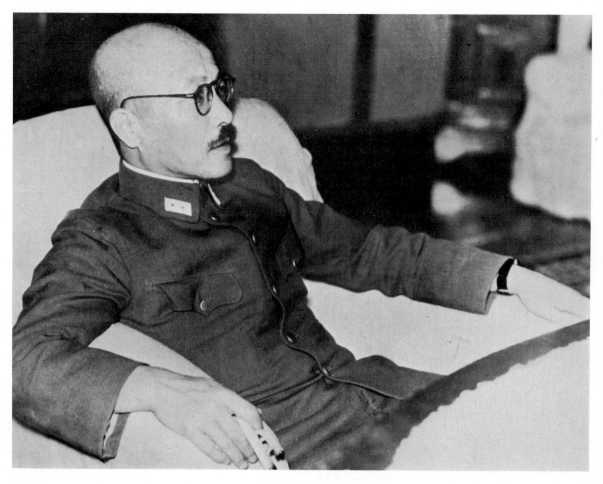

▷ *Tojo, Premier and War Minister of Japan, relaxes in his days of power. An authoritarian, his military dictatorship earned him the nickname of the "Razor".*
▷▷ *Tojo makes his deposition against the prosecution on January 6, 1948. The defendants claimed that mistakes and misunderstandings had arisen from inadequate translation facilities.*

General Hideki Tojo, Minister of War from July 1940 and Premier from October 1941. The Tribunal found that he bore "major responsibility for Japan's criminal attacks on her neighbours" and that "the barbarous treatment of prisoners and internees was well known to Tojo". Up to the fall of his cabinet in 1944 he connived at the orders which stated that sick prisoners should not be fed, because they could not work. He advocated the use of prisoners to build the Burma-Siam railway and ignored the high death rate. Hanged.

in court as to whether the initiation or waging of wars of aggression were punishable.

The idea of prosecuting the Axis leaders for crimes against peace did not arise until late on in the war. Never before had engaging in aggressive warfare been the basis of a charge. Its inclusion was an important part of America's post-war policy to establish the criminal status in international law of aggressive war. This means that whenever a leader leads his country to war, he must not only consider that he may lose, but that if he does so, he and his top service personnel will be tried as criminals and probably executed.

The question that arises at this point is that if waging aggressive war was not a crime at the outbreak of World War II, how could anybody be found guilty of it at this time? Can there be any crime without pre-existing laws which state that certain actions are criminal? Some say that there is no crime, while others contend that the existence of a law prohibiting some courses of action is a safeguard against injustice, a moral principle, but that it is not a rule of law, and an act may be punished as a crime if it was clearly illegal in character at the time it was committed.

"Crimes against humanity" is another vague concept. Victims of inhumane acts or persecutions who are nationals of occupied territories are the victims of war crimes. But does this also apply to Hitler's persecution of the Jews inside Germany? Here, there was no "war", and hence no war crime. This is where the category of crimes against humanity becomes important.

Definitions

This leads us on to the question of definitions. How did the trials define war crimes, and crimes against humanity?

The Nuremberg Charter defines war crimes as violations of the laws of war, including murder, ill-treatment, or the deportation for slave labour or for any other purpose of the civilian population of an occupied territory; the murder or ill-treatment of prisoners-of-war; the killing of hostages; plunder, wanton destruction of cities, towns or villages; and devastation not justified by military necessity.

Crimes against humanity included murder, extermination, enslavement, deportation, and other inhumane acts committed against any civilians before or during war;

3077

General Yoshijiro Umezu, commander-in-chief of the Kwantung Army from 1939 to July 1944, when he became Chief of the Army General Staff until the end of the war. No evidence was found to implicate him in any war crimes against P.O.W.s and internees. However, overwhelming evidence showed that he had conspired to wage aggressive war against China and the Western Powers. Appeared as a defence witness for Yamashita. Life imprisonment.

Shigenori Togo, Foreign Minister from October 1941 to September 1942 and during the last few months before the surrender. At these periods he was able to influence Japanese Government policy. The tribunal found therefore that he was not responsible for any war crimes either of neglect or commission, but found him guilty of conspiring to wage an aggressive war. Sentenced to 20 years imprisonment with effect from May 3, 1946.

Admiral Osami Nagano, Chief of the Navy General Staff. He urged the attack on Pearl Harbor after he realised that Japan was exhausting her fuel stocks. Resigned under pressure from Tojo in February 1944. He retired to private life and only reappeared for the Tokyo trials where he was charged with conspiring to wage an aggressive war. His death from a complex of infirmities in January 1947 while the trial was in progress caused headlines.

General Akira Muto, one time Chief of the Military Affairs Bureau and in 1945 chief-of-staff in the Philippines. Commanded the 2nd Imperial Guards Division from April 1942 to October 1944. He was held responsible for the starvation, torture, and murder of military and civilian detainees and for "gross breaches of the Laws of War." His claim of ignorance was described as "incredible". Partially responsible for the "Rape of Nanking". Hanged.

and the persecution on religious, racial, or political grounds in execution of or in connection with any crime within the jurisdiction of the tribunal, whether or not in violation of the domestic law of the country where perpetrated.

This last phrase has caused disquiet amongst critics of the trials, as it seemingly gives nations the right to interfere, in certain circumstances, in the internal affairs of another state. The I.M.T. considered crimes such as the German persecution of the Jews as acts of such heinous character that they clearly violated those principles of justice recognised by all civilised nations, and that under circumstances such as these, joint action by a group of states would be acceptable.

A further criticism of these definitions is that they were drawn up after the hostilities, by which time the Allies knew of what the Axis Powers were guilty.

Others have criticised the trials as a legal front for the Allies' desire for vengeance. Victor Gollancz, the British publisher, went so far as to call the trials "a comeback to barbarian ideas".

Apart from all the controversy as to whether or not the trials were legally justified, there are moral questions, too, to consider. It certainly does not seem right for the victors to sit in judgement over the vanquished, when the victors had certainly committed crimes similar to some of those for which they were now trying the vanquished. The definition of war crimes includes, as we have seen, devastation not justified by military necessity. When thinking of this, the Allied bombing of Dresden comes to mind.

The Allies right?

What right had the Allies to punish only the defeated Axis war criminals? Does victory wipe the slate clean?

It should be pointed out here that the I.M.T. did not consider aerial and submarine warfare. The court appears to have been convinced that German practices did not differ very greatly from Allied action in these areas . . . but it did not call them war crimes. This is illogical. All atrocities and horrors of war should have been dealt with, including the atom bombs dropped on Japan. Only the losers were

◁ *The courtroom scene in December 1946. The 28 leaders and alleged conspirators were described as "old" and "tired men". The trial lacked anyone of the colour of Göring, and was a curiously subdued affair. Only Tojo when he appeared in the dock had a "lynx-like, formidable face".*
▽ *A Shinto priest offers prayers for the return of Japanese P.O.W.s in Russia. Relatives of these men had invaded the Russian Embassy in Tokyo.*

△ *Late in 1952 two minor war criminals are released on parole. Yoshika Yagi (left), a former civilian employed by the Japanese Army and sentenced to 15 years, and Toshio Tatakeyama, a former colonel, sentenced to 12 years, leave Sugamo Prison.*

deemed guilty of waging aggressive war, war crimes, and crimes against humanity. The trials would have been better employed had they considered the course of the war as a whole, perhaps giving guidance on specific weapons and practices which should have been banned as inhumane and unlawful, regardless of their military value.

Retribution

It has been said that the trials had the sanction of the international community. Nineteen nations subscribed to the London agreement in addition to the four major powers. Therefore it was probably right politically to take jurisdiction over the Axis war leaders at the time. "Retribution" had been talked of so much during the war, that justice for the enemy war criminals became a major objective of the war,

and the trials were therefore expected. Public conscience demanded that the guilty be punished.

The United Nations affirmed the principles applied at Nuremberg, and thereby expressed their endorsement of the ruling of the court. This is tangible evidence that the principles of the Charter, as well as those in the judgement of the Tribunal, are valid in international law, and that their application was justified. The United Nations also instructed the Committee on the Codification of International Law to codify the principles laid down at Nuremberg.

It is no doubt desirable that the principles should be absorbed into international law. Every attempt to mitigate the horrors of war is welcome. But in the future, international law must be applied to all combatants, not just the vanquished. It is morally wrong for one side to be the victor, prosecutor, judge, and executioner combined, as the Allies were at Nuremberg.